I'm Alive

by

LILY HOPKINS

All Royalties to CERCAN

I'm Alive
by
Lily Hopkins

Published by Changing Places Publications

First Edition October 1991

ISBN 0 9517671 0 0 (Paperback)

Typeset and Printed by Anteus Graphics (TU)
222, Tower Street, Century Building, Brunswick Business Park,
Liverpool L3 4BJ
Tel: 051 709 1560

Cover Design by Phil Cooper

*I dedicate this book to my beloved mother,
Elizabeth Donnelly, from whom I inherited my
straight tongue, stubborness, and determination*

Contents

		Page
	Forward	7
	Background	9
1)	*Genesis*	11
2)	*Home-Coming*	24
3)	*Headlines*	31
4)	*Devastation*	43
5)	*Introducing Politics*	47
6)	*Diary of July*	56
7)	*My Family*	75
8)	*Deja Vu*	83
9)	*Key Findings*	91
10)	*Glasgow Smiles Better*	100
11)	*Bridge-Building*	107
12)	*Busy, Busy*	117
13)	*Six Cities and Me*	128
14)	*Kilroy*	145
15)	*Justice*	150
16)	*'Blunder Report'*	154
	Afterword	167
	Authors Note	169
	Photographs	171

Foreword

When I sat down to put pen to paper, I found myself somewhat unsure of where to begin. I had a story to tell which I felt had important implications for all women. The problem was, it was rather a long tale spanning a period of almost four years. After much thought, I decided to cover the first months in reasonable detail and hopefully, the remainder would flow. My one regret is that I could not tell the story in its entirety, as this would have resulted in volumes.

I had to choose the events which, in my opinion were the most important or perhaps the most startling. Sadly, this meant that I could not cover the stories of the individual women. They had suffered so much and I would not insult them by 'squeezing' their stories into a small section of this book. I would very much like to tell their stories and I do have their permission, so maybe I will at a later date.

To the many people I have met, and who have helped me over the past years in different ways, I apologise for not being able to mention you. Again, I would have been unable here to do you justice.

I thank you all from the bottom of my heart for your help, whether great or small. I would have found my work so much more difficult without you.

I was unable to mention in detail my many trips to London, yet there is a lady who lives there, without who's help I would not have been able to make these trips. This lady is Catherine Lancaster, who provided me with free board, lodgings and much of my transport, while in her area.

My sincere thanks to Cathy and her lovely family. God bless you all.

Background

During 1987, 487 women were recalled by Liverpool Health Authority for further testing, treatment, and physical examination.

This followed the revelation that a mix-up had occurred at the Women's Hospital in Liverpool, where the smear tests were analysed.

The 911 women who were ultimately involved were those who had attended for a smear test from March 1983 to December 1985.

It was decided by the Department of Health, the Liverpool Health Authority and other officials, that an Internal Review would take place to discover if a mistake had been made.

There was a suspicion among the general public and the women involved that a private inquiry would result in a 'cover-up' and a 'white wash'. They therefore called for a public inquiry. This attracted a great deal of media attention, but despite the many requests, endorsed by the Community Health Council, a public inquiry was denied.

The Community Health Council were not allowed representation at the review and stated that they felt unable to carry out their duty as the 'patient's voice'.

The conclusion of the Internal Review was that:

"A massive error of professional judgement" had occurred, "for which they could offer no reasonable explanation".

Chapter 1

GENESIS

"Chris, Liz, Julie, Nicky, Jamie, Chrissie. Tea's on the table!"

Typical night in our house. Scuffles, screams and yells. The kids come piling down the stairs and around the table.

"Chris, will you come down before your tea gets cold?" My husband was always last at the table, excepting me, of course. As in most households, Mother is always last to sit down.

Great! Tea on my lap, our local evening newspaper. It was my bad habit to read the paper during my meal, smashing! Duties over until after tea.

I would read just the headlines, turning over the pages unless something caught my eye like the woman's page, problem page, and of course, my horoscope.

I had reached page four or five, I stopped. Something *had* caught my sub-conscious eye. What was it? About the cancer smear test? I hastily turned back to the front page. Yes, I was right. I stared at the heading - "500 city women in Cancer Check."

I read and re-read the article. MY GOD! I was one of them. Was I one of them? I couldn't take my eyes off the print.

Oh, Please God, NO!

CANCER, CANCER, CANCER. The word seemed to have grown bigger than the surrounding print. I was going to *die*.

It all made sense now. The duplicated letter, the Health Woman's visit, the evasion, everything. My heart was thumping. I will never forget that feeling for as long as I

live.
I started suddenly and realised with horror, '500 women', it wasn't just me! I could not believe what I was reading. I felt as though my brain had seized up. I couldn't think. I could hear my husband's voice and the children chattering somewhere in the distance.
"Calm down," I told myself, "start at the beginning. What makes you think that you are one of these women?"
I read the article yet again.
'Women's Hospital....Smear Test mistake....Tests carried out between March 1983 and December 1985'.
It all fitted, I was one of them!
It is difficult to describe my feelings of sheer terror and blind panic. I felt that my whole body was encased in a narrow, sealed tube which had one small opening, and through that opening, I could see the barrel of a loaded gun. The gun however did not contain a bullet, it contained CANCER. To me at that moment, it was a more certain killer than a bullet could ever be, and if you think I am being over-dramatic, just ask anyone who has had cancer how they felt when they first found out. It *was* more dramatic for me because I had found out from a newspaper article.
I cast my mind back to 26th February, 1987. I had received a letter from the Medical Officer of Health for Liverpool. It stated that I may require further testing following my smear test taken in the summer of 1984. I really didn't think too much about it at that time. I was advised to ring for an appointment, which I did, and must admit to some surprise at receiving one for the 28th., two days away. That *was* quick.
The next day, on the 27th, I received another letter, identical to the first, but from my G.P. Later, that same day, a Health Visitor called at my home. She asked if I had

received the letter and impressed upon me the importance of keeping the appointment. I vaguely remember asking why she had called, but I don't recall her reply. I do know she did not tell me anything I didn't already know, which was precious little, and although she was a pleasant enough woman, I sensed an aura of....what? I didn't know. After she had gone I remarked to my husband, "no wonder the N.H.S. is short of money, they do everything in triplicate." We both laughed, little knowing what was to follow.
I went along to the Women's Hospital on the 28th, as arranged, and was shown into a small waiting room. I wasn't there very long when a doctor came in and after introducing himself, he asked me to follow him to the examination room. He asked me some routine question, presumably to check his records, and then asked to me to 'place' myself onto a 'funny looking' chair. I say 'place' myself because the chair had no bottom. I had certainly never seen one before, but then I had never visited a gynaecolocal clinic before, not even for a smear test which had been carried out in Family Planning, or Ante-Natal clinics. Not that I thought very much about having smears. I had always been very healthy. I attended, when asked, as a matter of routine. I had never asked why they were doing smears taken at an ante-natal clinic during my third pregnancy. As most women who have had babies will verify, you don't ask questions. The doctor will say "lie down, sit up" or "dress, undress", "legs up, legs down". We don't ask why, we just do as we are told, after all, they know what they are doing. Anyway, I climbed up onto 'the chair' and the doctor took a smear. Then he said that he was going to look at my cervix through the colposcope. A what? He told me that a colposcope was really only "binoculars on legs with a light attachment" which enabled him to view the tissue more closely. He said he could see

"two small wart-like lesions" whatever that was, and that he would take a tiny piece of tissue for further testing. This hurt a little bit. I was told I could get down now, and a nurse helped me. As I was climbing down, I remarked to them both that the chair looked like a dentist chair without a bottom, no one even smiled. I thought: "miserable lot". I think I was chattering on a bit, to hide my nerves, probably. The doctor said I would probably have to be admitted to hospital to have these two 'wart-like lesions' removed. I would be kept in for four or five days. He said I should return in two weeks for the results. I agreed I would.

I did not ask any questions, because I would not have known what kind of questions to ask. Anyway, why should I ask questions? The doctors knew what they were doing. I certainly didn't.

I returned to hospital two weeks later as requested, and what happened there *did* make me feel uneasy. Not so much what was said but rather the atmosphere and the way *they* were behaving.

I was seen by a doctor in what seemed to be a room used to store and prepare dressings, you know, lots of shelves and a work top.

I was asked to sit down. The doctor perched himself on the work top, and the nurse was leaning against the wall with her arms folded. She was sort of looking down. Looks were passing back and forth between them. I had seen those looks before, when we were called to a hospital in 1984 after a fire at the home of my parents-in-law. When the family were gathered together, a doctor and nurse came in and this 'look' passed between them, almost as though they were saying silently: "Lets get it over with".

They had bad news for us as my mother-in-law had died in the fire. This was the kind of vibes I was getting now. The doctor began to speak hesitantly, at first, and then he told me I would need to come in for 'the small operation'. And that if I didn't have the lumps removed now, I may need a 'bigger' operation later. He was saying something else but I couldn't concentrate. I looked over at the nurse, but she still had her eyes down-cast. Somehow the words did not match with the looks. I became aware he was still speaking....“sent for sooner”....“came back sooner”, I don't know, but as I usually do when faced with a difficult situation, I adopted my optimistic pose. I am a great believer in facing up to problems with a smile. Does that make sense? I have always found it helps, although it can be misunderstood. He ended the interview by telling me I would receive a letter informing me when to come for a pre-operative assessment, to check I was fit for a general anaesthetic. Ooh, that was scary! I rose from the seat to go, and I said with a smile, “better late than never.” If only I had known. The nurse muttered something under her breath. I heard only the “ugh”. I looked back at the doctor. Both now had their eyes down. I frowned and thought “funny lot”. I left the hospital feeling very shaky. I suppose because of my forthcoming operation. I felt as though they had held something back. The whole episode seemed a bit strange, but I put it down to my own nerves. Hospitals' atmospheres can make you feel a bit funny, can't they?

When I got home, I was still feeling a little nervy. I told myself to stop acting like a baby. It was only a small op, to remove a couple of little lumps, “the size of a pin-head” the doctor had said. I put it out of my mind and succeeded quite well. I would not worry at least until nearer the time.

My first two visits had been to the Women's Hospital. I now had been asked to attend the Royal Liverpool Hospital for my pre-op. assessment.

I was determined this time to ask some questions, but quite

honestly, I hadn't a clue. I had learned that the smear test was a cancer test, but that had nothing to do me. I only had 'two small, wart-like lumps' - that wasn't cancer. I would ask about that too. It would make me feel better, I think?
The doctor examined my chest and back, he then felt my tummy. He wouldn't examine my breasts because I was still having my period.
He explained that I would be admitted on 6th May, and that I would have my operation the next day.
This doctor seemed more authoritative than the others I had seen, and he spoke more clearly. I do not wish to imply criticism of the first two doctors, or the nurse, as I later found out they had been left to 'clean up the mess'.
I uttered the dreaded words: "Have I got cancer?"
He replied: "No, no."
He more or less then repeated what the first two had said. I asked him about the operation. He said he had never known it to fail. That was something I hadn't thought of - *failure*. I suppose with him putting it into my mind, I went on to ask: "What happens if it does fail?"
He said I would then need to have a hysterectomy. I knew that meant removal of the womb, but not much more. Anyway, it wouldn't come to that. Hadn't he just said it rarely failed.
I left the hospital with a shaky feeling inside although I may have appeared calm. My stomach felt just like jelly, so did my legs. I was nervous about the operation, but I didn't have cancer, so that was alright.
I read about the blunder again. A feeling of great anger came over me. What the heck was going on? The article stated that no one needed surgery, only out-patient treatment. That was a lie! I had been told, only yesterday, that I needed an operation. I decided to ring the newspaper.
I jumped up. I remember my husband asking what was

wrong and recall shouting rather wildly, that it was a big lie. I raged into the hall and rang directory enquiries for the number. My hand was shaking as I dialled the digits. I do not know whether it was with anger or with nerves. I was terrified. I had never spoken to a reporter before. The thought was quite daunting. Was I doing the right thing? Then I remembered the lies. To hell with it, there was something wrong with me and I just had to find out what. The doctors weren't going to tell me, otherwise they would have done so during one of my three visits. Who else could I contact. No! it had to be the newspaper.

A man answered the phone. I asked to speak to the lady reporter who had written the article. I was told that she wasn't there at that time, but the man asked if he could help. Perhaps that was his mistake because for the next two or three minutes he must have felt like his ears were dropping off. I poured out all my frustrations, fears, anger, and bewilderment. I suppose it might have sounded as though I was blaming the paper. Of course I wasn't. I just had to let it out. Besides I would not have known at that time, who to blame for what.

He let me ramble on for a while. I think he realised from the tenor of the conversation, that I was terrified. My voice was shaking. After a few moments, he said something like: "Calm down, you sound as though you have had a shock. Would you like to tell me your side of the story?" I felt slightly better having got that lot off my chest. I explained about the article and why I thought I was one of the women. Also about my visits to the hospitals, the lot. He asked if I would allow my story to be published, I was unsure about that. He explained that the article was a statement made by the Health Authority, and that the paper had printed it in order to trace the 'missing women'.

I thought if I don't give my penny'orth, then no one will

know the truth. I asked if I could make a a statement anonymously? He replied that it may not have so much 'clout', but if that was the way I felt, then he would be happy to comply with my wishes. He took down a few particulars and handled me with great sensitivity. He instinctively knew that I was still in shock. He did not try to make me say anything that I did not want to say. That was my first experience of Steve Harrison, and in my opinion, he is still the greatest reporter. With no disrespect to any other reporters, but I got to know Steve first. This may sound silly, but I trusted Steve straight away, and that was unusual for me. I am normally very wary of people until I get to know them. Steve did not let me down. He has always been honest with me, and if I were to ask him not to print then he would still respect my wishes. He said my story would appear in the paper the next day.

As I replaced the hand-set, I again began to have doubts as to the wisdom of speaking to the press. You hear such tales, don't you. I need not have worried, the story was told exactly the way I had related it, not one extra word. It appeared in both the morning and evening paper (they were 'sister papers'). I wasn't too sure what I expected the outcome to be as I was still quite confused, but I do know that I was scared stiff to go out that day. I wondered if people would guess it was me, that "Mother of four from Fazakerley".

I actually had five children, but I remember going on about dying and leaving my four young children. My 'first baby' was twenty-four. The others were sixteen and under. When I finally plucked up the courage to venture out in the street, no one took any notice of me. Thank God for that. I do not know if I could have coped, at that time with people talking about my story or even the issue in general.

It is now May 3rd. Have two months really gone by? I got

the letter on February 26th, and attended hospital for the first time on the 28th, then again on April 27th. Then the article in the newspaper on the 28th. I was in a state of suspense, not knowing whether I was coming or going. I would wake up in the morning and look at the kids. Time was marching on, it would soon be my time. What could I do to protect the kids? The two older girls might have managed, but what about my three babies. They were just babies, at four, nine and twelve. I was beginning to panic. Who could I speak to? I was convinced that I would not wake up from the anaesthetic. Sounds crazy now, but then, it was was only too real.

Jamie, my only son. I had waited so long for him, and little Chrissie. I would hate to leave her behind. She was my 'problem pregnancy'. She weighed in at only 3lb 13 ozs, and twelve inches long. She was still a little china doll. Then there was Nicky, at twelve. She would soon need a mother to talk to. Oh God, what could I do. Liz and Julie would miss me too, and my Chris?

I tried to reason with the situation. Hang on, perhaps I should see a solicitor, that was what victims of mistakes do! I wasn't after financial recompense, I didn't think I would be here to spend it. But if there was compensation, it would surely help the children. My husband is not an academic type, so I decided that I would have to sort it out before I went.

All sorts of things were going through my mind, but I thought, yes, that is the answer.

I picked up the phone book. Crikey, there were so many solicitors. I wasn't so sure about this idea. Could I talk to a man? Most solicitors *are* men. Then one of my brothers said he knew of a lady solictor. He gave me her number and she agreed to visit me at home. Perhaps because I sounded so distressed, or perhaps because I was going into hospital

very soon.
Helen Barry came into my life. She called the evening before I went into hospital. She listened to my story. She had of course read about the 'mix-up' in the press, but I think maybe I was her first smear case client. She was very sympathetic and I felt a kinship with her as I had with Steve. Colette accompanied Helen. They were colleagues, and I was surprised to learn that I had met her when she was a little girl, and that I knew her family.
Helen took my statement and asked me to sign it. I tried to impress upon her that she must proceed with my case, even if I didn't come through it, for the family. I knew nothing about the law and did not realise that if I had died, it would have been up to my husband, as next-of-kin.
Helen said I should concentrate on getting better, that she would see me when I came home, and that she would send for my medical records.
For the reminder of the evening, we watched some T.V. and chatted a bit, but generally we were tense. We didn't seem to know what to say to each other and yet for me, although I was tense, I was also dreadfully calm. It was not a pleasant feeling. More like I had accepted the inevitable. My suitcase was already packed. Everything was ready. I suppose this is how people have felt when awaiting execution.
My husband and I did not speak very much. Not really speak. Words passed between us but they had no real meaning. I think it was quite late when we went to bed. Even the children had stayed up late. We didn't say much in bed either. We just cuddled up close and went to sleep. Sleep came quickly, which surprised me, but I expect I was mentally exhausted.
We got up at about the usual time next morning. Got the kids ready and out to school. I wanted everything to be

'normal'. I gave them all a nice big kiss and cuddle, but as I watched them go I felt awful.

They did not know, you see. No one did. I had told no one that I was going to die. Not that anyone had actually said I was going to die, but in my mind it was confirmed.

Maybe I should have talked about my condition to the family, but how could I? I didn't know myself. All I knew was that cancer kills. My smear test had gone wrong, it was a cancer test, and so that was that. I believed this was the reason why the doctors had said nothing to me about the mistake. Well they don't tell you when you're going to die, although I often wondered if they had told my husband, but I did not have the guts to ask him. I'm not too sure whether I was trying to protect him, or myself.

We left for the hospital at about 1.50pm, a bit neat with the timing but this was the one occasion when I didn't mind if I was a little late.

The staff were very nice. They welcomed us onto the ward. Visiting time was half way through, but they let my husband stay longer. Someone brought us both a nice cup of tea. Funny the things you remember. We just sat looking at one another, making small talk but not really speaking. I should imagine that our minds were full of questions but neither wanted to say anything in case it upset the other. Most of my conversation revolved around the family. Do this, don't do that. Buy this, get that.

We had been sitting like this for about one hour. I could tell he was feeling very uncomfortable, so I said: "Maybe you'd better go. I'll walk you down to the ward door."

He rose and we walked out arm in arm. When we reached the door, we held each other tight and had a good kiss and cuddle.

He said: "I'll see you tomorrow."

The children were to visit me that evening. I looked at him

and slowly said: "Yes, but don't come in the afternoon. I may still be groggy. Ring up during visiting and they will tell you how I am.'' Really I didn't want him to come in, just in case *it* happened. I mean it would be awful to come to the hospital with flowers and goodies and have to take them back home. Oh, the things I thought of then. It gives me the creeps now to remember.

I had taken some books in with me to keep myself busy, but mostly I just smoked my head off.

I got talking to a lady who had been admitted at the same time.

I'll call her 'Paula'. She told me she was in for the same operation. She looked worried. She was asking a lot of 'what if's'. I told her not to worry, it was only a little op. Here was me, convinced I was going to die, telling her to relax. I couldn't tell her the 'truth' now could I? Well I mean....you just don't tell people things like that right before an op, do you?

'Big O day'. The nurse woke us at six for a light early breakfast, tea with a slice of toast, and then we went back to sleep until eight. We both got up and went for a shower, after our smoke of course. Round about ten, or was it twelve? the nurse came with our pre-meds. We were told not take the tablets until we were in bed. We went for one last smoke, and then got into bed and took our dose.

It didn't seem to work straight away, and so I decided to read for a while. I soon began to feel drowsy, sort of floating, cloud nine stuff. I put my book down, and as I was drifting off I thought, it will just be like going to sleep. I felt very relaxed and peaceful. The next thing I knew, the porter had arrived to 'take me down, I was awake but still very groggy.

In the operating theatre ante-room, where they get you asleep, the 'gas man', I called him, asked me if I liked

garlic as he was inserting the needle.
I replied: "Oh, yes, I lo-o-o...."
I became aware of 'clinking' noises, I could feel a niggling pain in my back. I was in blackness. I thought, I musn't be dead yet, and then I drifted off.
My next recollection was of a distant voice. I tried to open my eyes. I could see three nurses, all floating. They were saying something.
I opened my eyes and stared straight ahead. My body felt very heavy. Someone was sitting beside my bed. I couldn't move my head but my eyes followed the feeling in my hand. My husband was there and he was holding my hand. My brain wasn't working yet. I was still having odd notions of floating nurses, but they were gone. Hang on, I'm sitting up, nearly. I looked at my husband again and found that I could move my head. My month was dry, I swallowed, I said: "Hi". I learned later that the 'floating nurses' had washed my hands and face, and propped me up to make me more comfortable.
'Floating nurses' - is that why they call them angels? I don't remember any of that.
Yes, I said 'hi' to my husband, but what I really meant was "I'm alive, I'm alive!"
If I had been able to I would have jumped out of the bed, operation gown and all, and run round the ward screaming *"I'm alive"*.

Chapter 2

HOMECOMING

"Mrs. Hopkins, ...Mrs Hopkins, would you like a cup of tea? Do you take sugar dear?"
I stirred. I manoeuvered myself into a sitting position, and slowly, gingerly, lowered my frame onto the bed. Would it hurt? The anaesthetic had worn off. I had not had any pain-killers today. What about stitches? My back ached but I wasn't in too much pain 'underneath'. I wanted to go to the loo, would that hurt? How little we knew - women, I mean. We know absolutely nothing about our bodies.
A nurse came into the ward, I asked if I could get up. She said she would ask. The answer was 'yes', and so I carefully swung my legs over the side of the bed, holding on to the bedside cabinet for support. My feet touched the ground. So far so good. My slippers were inside the cabinet so I had to bend down, ever so slowly. I felt rather foolish, like a wooden puppet, but you can't be too careful, no point in taking chances. I wished I had asked more questions about it afterwards. I didn't like to trouble the nurses as they were already very busy.
"Oh well", I thought, picking up my toiletry bag and my ciggies, armed and ready. "Here we go", and made for the toilet.
When I first 'sat down', I was afraid to 'let go'. It stung a bit at first, but then it was alright.
That over, I had a wash. I wondered at the wisdom of having a smoke but I was gasping. I decided to sit down

'Paula' was there. I learned that she was also one of the recalls, as the ladies involved in the mix-up were known. We talked at some length. She asked me what my solicitor had said. She worked in a hospital, and was afraid to say too much in case she put her job at risk. I suggested she have a chat with a solicitor and explained that she would not be forced to continue with her case if she did not want, but she would find out the facts before deciding. She took Helen's number.

That afternoon, when the doctors were making their rounds, I asked my consultant how the operation had gone.

"Very well", she replied. If, when my vaginal pack had been removed I was not bleeding too heavily, I could go home next day. Vaginal pack? What on earth was that?

Later that day, a nurse came to remove my pack. I learned that after some gynaecological operations, they pack the vagina with fine gauze, like a narrow bandage. The gauze is soaked in an antiseptic solution to promote healing and prevent infections.

She removed it with small forceps. It was rather like spaghetti, yards and yards of it. It wasn't very painful, more of a stinging sensation, but it brought tears to my eyes. The nurse said everything looked fine and that there was not a lot of bleeding. I could look forward to going home.

I felt almost light-headed, I was going home. I had only been in hospital for three days at that time. It felt much longer. The cloud on my horizon was the backache. I had mentioned it to the staff, but they hadn't really said much. I reasoned that it was probably caused by the operation, and that it would go in a day or two. The thing that worried me was that I remembered when, as a child, I had overheard my Mum and Grannie talking about a neighbour who had died. My Mum was saying: "I knew she wouldn't last long when

I heard about her backache.'' I don't know what was wrong with the woman, only that she had undergone a 'woman's operation'. In those days, you didn't talk openly about 'womens things'.

My husband came to collect me next day. I had already packed my case as I was eager to get home to my family. 'Paula' had gone home that morning and she promised to keep in touch.

The staff at the hospital had not mentioned the 'mistake' and neither did I. I couldn't stop smiling. I was so happy. I giggled when I thought of the letter in my handbag, addressed to my solicitor and containing my 'Last Will' plus instructions to her to carry on with the case. My husband asked me what I was laughing at. I said: ''Nothing''.

I had been in hospital for two days following my operation. I was too hyped up to work on my Jesus book, but I had plenty of time to think and to make plans. I had decided to get all the information I could on abnormal smears, treatments and the patients' chances. (I did not use words like diagnosis, or prognosis in those days. I don't think I had even heard of them. It was to be another two or three months before I become 'professional'.)

On leaving the hospital, I was told to take it easy for seven days. I wasn't told why, but I would take their advice anyway. I later found out that there was a slight risk of haemorrhage after a cone biopsy.

It was great being home, the kids were glad to see me and made quite a fuss. I sent my eldest daughter out to buy me a medical encyclopaedia and a book on gynaeocolgical nursing, plus four books from the library. I set about my studies. I was determined to know it all.

I pottered around the house but did not venture outdoors. I read a lot and learned quickly about the smear test and

abnormal smears, from the patients' point of view. I was beginning to find my feet.
Thursday, 14th May, seven days since my op. I could go out today. I was childishly excited about that. My family thought I was going crackers. I got the kids ready for school. Julie was in the sixth form, and Nichola was in the Juniors. They went by themselves. Chris, my husband took Jamie to Infant School and little Chrissie to morning nursery. I had a wash and got dressed. Now where shall I go? Not too far this time. Little did I know, fate had other plans for me.
I made a pot of tea and had just sat down when the phone rang. " Hello, my name is Mick Ord. I am the producer of *Town and Around* on *Radio Merseyside*."
WHAT! I thought. He asked to speak to Lily Hopkins.
"Speaking." I replied. He explained that they had heard of the smear test mix-up and wanted to "do something" on their programme.
I said: "Oh", wondering why were they ringing me? They wanted me to come to the studio for a discussion on the issue.
Me! on the radio? No, this can't be happening. My mouth went all dry. He was still talking. I didn't hear it all..... "How do you feel about what has happened to you?"
I replied that I was very angry about not being told by the proper authorities. I felt the red heat rise in my body, the way it did when I read the newspaper article. Would I come to the studio? I asked if I would have to give my name. I was still worried about doing that. I don't know why but I suppose it's a case of 'what will people think?' He asked me what I was going to do? Was I going to write to the Health Authority? To be honest, I really didn't know. I wouldn't get anything done if people didn't hear. It would have to be made public to have impact. He wasn't forceful,

quite the opposite. He was nice and sympathetic. He was telling me the same as the reporter, and it made sense. I realised that this was my chance, to do what? I felt that it was speak now or forever hold your tongue, and that was not me! So I said YES! I was going for it. I have often wondered that if I'd known then the outcome, would I still have 'gone for it'? I like to think that I would.

My husband returned from the school and I told him about the phone call. He was flabbergasted. He couldn't believe it, his wife on the radio.

They sent a taxi to pick me up. I was terribly nervous, worse than when I had spoken to the reporter. My voice, on the radio! I did not think about the thousands of people who might be listening, which is just as well, because I don't think I could have managed.

Mick met me at reception, took me through for a cuppa, and introduced me to the 'backroom boys and girls'. They could tell I was nervous and did their best to make me feel at ease. I was taken into the studio to meet Roger Philips, the presenter. What a lovely man. He has the brightest and most twinkly eyes you have ever seen, a real gent. He said that rather than have me make a statement, he would ask questions. I could then just answer as it would be easier for me. He explained that although I was allowed to tell the truth over the air, there were some things I would not be able to say, e.g. I could not make accusations without proof. What we agreed to do was if I was straying into 'dodgy' territory, he would wave his finger. I know nothing of the laws governing libel or slander, and as far as I was concerned a laboratory error would have been committed by people working in a lab. I didn't realise just how many people that covered - junior and senior staff, management, and consultant in charge. It was natural for me to want to tell the whole truth. I was very upset by the whole thing, but when you are nervous, the words don't necessarily come out correctly, or in the right order. I trusted Roger with his wide experience and he didn't let me down. He steered me through the one 'almost' mistaken choice of words, when I mentioned 'technicians'. He said that we could not attribute the blame to anyone yet as an investigation was being carried out. Of course I agreed. Roger, with his expertise, led me to cover the entire issue in a very short space of time, from the letter, discovery, treatment, outcome, promiscuity and ending with a piece about the other women involved. We suggested that they might like to contact me so that, basically, we could support each other. He said seeing as I had learned quite a lot about abnormal smears, that maybe I could help the others to understand. I knew what I had been through, as a result of 'not knowing', and so I readily agreed. My telephone number was given, and I went home.

At home, Chris and Liz were in chaos. Apparently, as soon as my number was mentioned, the phone started to ring. They both handled it very well. It could not have been easy, especially since they were not prepared. I don't think anyone realised just how much the women needed help and support. The medical side had been taken care of, but no one had considered the trauma.

There are those in the medical profession who claim that having a positive smear result would cause trauma in any woman, but who can say that it was no different for the recalled women? Let me ask you one question.....How would *you* like to learn that you have a potentially killer disease from the newspapers, or from a radio news bulletin?

No, it was far more traumatic for the recall women, not only for the above reason, but because they had been led to believe that their tests were clear.

The phone was still ringing when I arrived home half an

hour later. We took 32 calls that day. Some of the women had spoken to the press, one or two had been interviewed by the radio and television news people, but now we were together, a body of women, not just an odd woman here or there. We would make plans for the truth and justice.

That really was the start of my help-line. As time went by, women who were not affected by the blunder rang for advice or support. That help-line is still going today, and will continue until no one calls for help.

Chapter 3

HEADLINES

After the radio broadcast, things really hotted up! I was being contacted almost daily by the press, and gave several radio news interviews. The other women had also started to make press statements and we were getting headlines like.......
"CANCER TEST SCANDAL"
"100 Women told 'We got it wrong.' "

"MY CANCER TEST NIGHTMARE."
"Agony of Mum who the doctors said was safe."

"LET MY UNBORN BABY LIVE."
"Smear mum urged. Have a abortion."

"SECRET TESTS REVEAL CANCER BLUNDER".

During this time, I was studying hard. I had learned as much as was possible from the patients' point of view, but now I needed to know more.
If I wanted to change the system, I had to learn to converse with doctors in their 'own language'. I had always been interested in medical matters because I had once wanted to be a nurse. I was put off this by a friend who was a student nurse. She told me such horrible stories about the 'activities' of dead bodies. There was no way I could have coped with that, or so I thought. I have regretted my cowardice ever since.

Through my 'Jesus studies', I was used to Latin and Greek. This helped a lot when I came to peruse the real medical stuff.

I need to think like doctors, know what they knew. In other words, view the patient from the other side of the bed.

Some of the women were very confused about what was happening to them, and if I wanted to help them understand - and I did - then first I had to understand.

My struggle for knowledge began. The more I studied, the greater my thirst.

Chris and the kids were very good in those early days. It must have been difficult for them living with me, my nose permanently stuck in books.

I was surprised to find that I could absorb information so quickly. I was like a sponge, I soaked it up.

Before the cancer thing, I was hoping to return to college to study ancient religion, history and theology. I must admit to being a bit worried as to my ability to learn. It was many a long year since I left school. Also, I wasn't getting any younger.

Oh, I didn't feel my age. I used to think of myself as being 'sensibly young', or, in the last flush of youth, certainly not middle aged. I suppose I was, at least approaching middle age. But you are as young as you feel and I felt young.

I did, however, realise that my brain cells may 'feel their age'. I was pleased to discover that they apparently did not. I was brighter, keener, and sharper than I had been in my youth, but now I had a much stronger motivation.

They wouldn't tell us what we wanted to know, so with a lot of luck, and by the grace of God, *they* wouldn't have to.

Yes, I was definitely a bore at home. All I could think of was cervical cancer, abnormal smears, treatments, and books, books, books.

The help-line was going strong, it was my only connection

with the other women at that time. I had been in touch with Pat Kirwan, the young mum who doctors said was 'safe'. She was a great help. She was also in touch with the recalled women and did a lot of telephone work. She would usually pass them on to me so that we could combine our efforts.

Poor Pat, her own life had been screwed up, and yet she was helping others. Pat had been a bit 'Agoraphobic?, but was responding well to treatment. Now, with the additional strain of the blunder, she was right back where she started, or even worse. She wouldn't go out without her husband, Jimmie. She was afraid of having a panic attack.

Next, a woman called Pauline Barrows contacted me. Like Pat and myself, she was worried sick. She was in touch with quite a few women from her own area, and like Pat, she would refer them on to be 'networked'. We knew that there was strength and support in numbers. Pauline was having a bad time herself but she willingly joined the 'crew'.

Late in May, we learned, again via the press, that there was to be an inquiry into the blunder, or 'mix-up' as the authorities called it. This was to be held in private and they were calling it 'an Internal Review.'

They really were the limit. First they didn't tell us that we were victims of a mistake, then they had the nerve to hold the inquiry in private. Did we not have the right to know what was happening with our bodies? Did we not also have the right to know what had gone wrong? We were not really asking at that time 'whodunnit?' I don't think we fully understood the implications, and so didn't know whether it would be one person, or a number of people, or even if that mattered. We were scared stiff because it was out of our control, and there was no one in authority we felt able to trust. We were going back and forth to our doctors and hospitals, and no matter how nice the doctors were, we were looking for ulterior motives in everything they said. If they were nice, we thought our condition was more serious than it was. If they were not nice, we didn't like that either. We were in a 'no win' situation and so were the doctors. The whole affair had been handled very badly, leaving us with no faith in our doctors.

Pat, Pauline and I discussed the possibility of one of us being present at the inquiry, and it was decided that I would write to the Chair of the Liverpool Health Authority to ask if I could attend.

I received a reply a few days later from a Mr. Criddle, who was head of Administration saying that it would not be possible for me to attend as the Internal Review was to be held in private. The letter went on to say that the 'key issues' would be published in due course.

To say we were angry was certainly an understatement. Together we devised a plan of action. We would contact some of the other women and hold a peaceful demonstration outside the Royal Liverpool Hospital where the inquiry was to be held.

We were joined in this plan of action by Maria Partington, a lady who had appeared on television after learning from a radio broadcast that she was one of us. She was just as angry as we were.

Helen Barry had introduced me to Margaret Thompson, secretary of the Commmunity Health Council. Margaret was a very nice woman, but I was wary of her. After all, the CHC is just an extension or another department of the Health Authorities. At least as none of us had heard of them, that is what we thought. Basically, we didn't trust anyone with 'health' in their title.

Margaret told us that Linda Pepper, Vice-chair of the council, was being allowed in to the inquiry as an observer. I also met Sylvia Hikins, the Chair. She and Linda worked closely together.

I visited the CHC quite a lot in the days that followed and got to know the three women quite well. They were nice. It was a pity they were on the wrong side. Then, as though to prove me wrong, we received the news that Linda was not going to be allowed in to the inquiry after all.

The Health Authority issued the following statement by way of explanation:

"Solicitors for some of the witnesses objected, saying clients might not be prepared to discuss their cases in front of outsiders......"

Now that said it all. Outsiders, indeed. Just who the heck did these people think they were? We were no outsiders. Our lives had been placed on the line. Anyway, what did they have to say that worried them so?

The CHC were furious at not being allowed in, and I began to realise that they really were on 'our side'. They were not part of the health authority.

Sylvia and Linda gave a television interview where they stated publicly that they were disgusted at the treatment of the recalled women, and said that they were gravely concerned by the enormous scale of the blunder. Also they were mystified by the refusal to allow Linda observer status as promised. They felt that an independent body should have been there to represent the public interests.

We felt good that the CHC agreed with our views, but I still maintained a slight suspicion. It later became obvious that my suspicions were unfounded. The CHC were very supportive to us, especially Margaret Thompson, and shortly after, Julie Bradley, but I'll tell you more about Julie as she enters the story.

It was a small peaceful demonstration, some of the women were either too ill to come out, or too shy. A few ran for cover when they saw the television cameras.

Those of us who braved it, more than made up for our numbers, including Pat's husband, Jimmie, and her little son, James, who was entralled by all the attention. Patients who were attending the Royal, and visitiors stopped to look. Also, some of the staff came out to have a look. I think I can safely say, we received ample coverage.
Next morning headlines read:

'WOMEN'S DEMO FURY."

"'.........They were demanding a public inquiry because they fear the private hearing at the Royal Liverpool Hospital will be a "cover up". The angry protestors......waved banners saying 'Our bodies, our lives, why the secrecy?' "
One or two members of Parliament turned up to show their support, as by this time, the matter had been raised in the House of Commons and the Prime Minister had refused a public inquiry, saying that it would serve no useful purpose.
No useful purpose to who? It would have served the *victims* well to know what had happened. We were not going to be satisfied with an 'in camera' meeting. We had trusted them before and look where it got us. So we were not going to trust them again.
The Authority made several attempts at justification, but we did not, could not accept any of them. What it boiled down to, we felt, was that there was something to hide, otherwise why would witnesses be so afraid to assist the inquiry in the presence of observers? More to the point, why did their legal representatives feel that it was necessary to exclude 'outsiders'? It was all too 'cloak and dagger' for us to consider that the conclusion would be completely truthful, assuming, of course, that we were given access to the final report.
We decided that demonstrations were perhaps not enough,

and so we started to collect signatures to present to the Prime Minister, and to the Health Authority.
There were about 58 women taking legal action against the Authority for alleged medical negligence. Our solicitors were highly suspicious of the apparent 'cloak of secrecy', statements made, and interviews given by them, were sensibly guarded. In any case, they were still awaiting our medical records, and could proceed no further until they had access.
There was much hustle and bustle at home. I was busy preparing for the forthcoming marriage of our daughter, Liz. I was to make her dress, and the bridesmaids' dresses. Julie, our second daughter would help with the maids, but I wanted to do the bride's dress myself. Like all mothers, I had looked forward to the day when one of my 'chicks' would wed. I wanted to do everything, but it didn't quite work out that way.
First of all, we had to delay the wedding because of my May operation. (It should have been in June.) Now it was planned for August, and nothing was going to stop it this time.
I was still waiting for my results, but I knew, deep down that it had been unsuccessful. Call it second sight, or intuition, what ever you like, but I *knew!*
I didn't tell the family of my thoughts as they had been through enough. Time to worry when 'my thoughts' were confirmed. I wanted to keep things in perspective, if possible. I also knew that although there was still a chance of me dying, it would not be right away. Not like I had imagined at the beginning. I would have some time, and I was going to make doubly sure that I was being driven on by a force I didn't even understand, I had no control over it. I was determined to see this through.
Helen rang to say that she had received my medical records

and that she would like to call on me later that day.
I knew that she would have bad news, I just *knew*!
Chris, my husband, was getting ready to go to the post office to collect his Giro Cheque. He brought Helen a cup of coffee before going out.
Helen made no attempt to open her brief case, she made light conversation and slowly drank her coffee. She said we should wait for Chris to return and then she could talk to us together. I didn't want Chris to hear before I had the chance to 'digest' the information. I was also anxious to 'get it over with' before the kids came home from school. She was obviously not keen to tell me on my own, and so I looked at her and said: "Helen, I *know*!"
She asked me if I had been speaking to the doctors. I replied I hadn't. She looked at me, feeling deeply for me, and finally opened her brief case.
She began, reluctantly to hand over the documents saying: "I still think you would be better to wait until Chris returns."
I almost snatched the papers from her hand. She took no offence at my actions. She knew I was emotionally strong and that I would not have taken the papers if there was a chance of me not, at least initially, being able to handle the situation. I truly appreciated her genuine concern, and enhanced my feeling of trust in her. It was good to be able to trust someone.
There it was....
"....around almost the whole cervix, ...amounting in most parts to *Carcinoma-in-Situ*....involvement of the gland crypts.... extends well into the canal.... excision is *incomplete*."
The operation had failed. I was now looking towards a hysterectomy.
I knew by this time that a Carcinoma-in-Situ does not kill,

what was really worrying me was, had they told the truth? Were they holding something back because of the blunder?
The Authorities claimed that they were being very open about what was happening, well not in our eyes. While they weren't exactly telling lies, they *were* holding back. They were not telling us all, and to us, the women, that was just the same. So, while 'knowing' is one thing, having it confirmed is quite another. I was shocked, scared, and totally devastated. But, I could not show my feelings, not to Helen not Chris, and definitely not to the kids.
I made light of the situation, saying: "Oh well, it looks like I'm going for the *big* one".... "They are not getting me on the table until after the wedding".
On a more serious note, I said to the family that they were not to worry. At worst, I would need to have a hysterectomy. My secret thoughts were, "If it has not gone too far."
Nothing was going to spoil Liz's wedding. She had been a good daughter and I wanted her to have a day to remember.
I was due to return to the hospital in a few days for my 'official results', and I was glad that I had seen my medical records before going, as I'm afraid that I could not trust the doctors to tell me the truth. This was very unfair on the doctor. My consultant had not made a mistake. She probably had nothing to do with smear tests as such. I was suspicious of all medics. Like the other women, my faith in the medical profession, was *zero*.
Helen, of course, did exactly the right thing in showing me my records. She knew, even in those early days, that I was the type of person who needs to know. She also realised that I was a sensible, level-headed sort. She was aware that if I had needed Chris's support, I would have said so.
What I needed at that time was to be alone, to collect my thoughts, and to summon up my courage.

There was a good chance there would only be a few cancer cells left, but there was equal chance that it might have spread. I had to know it all if I were to take stock and remain in control.

When I was alone, I reasoned with myself. I argued and counselled myself. I have always been able to do that with any problems life has brought. I would cope.

I couldn't help thinking about cancer and what a terrible disease it was, even if it is the kind that they can cure. Just the word still sends shivers down my spine. I wish to hell they could find a cure.

Although I seem to have the gift of getting others to talk about their fears and worries, I cannot do it myself. I have never been able to. Maybe because I 'discuss it with myself' I don't feel the need that others might feel. Also, I have always been a very self confident person. I was quite happy to share my physical worries with the other women, but not my mental anguish. Although I felt like I had been to hell and back, I would cope. Maybe I should have been a doctor. I'm coldly 'clinical' enough.

I find it hard even writing about my inner feelings, but I promised to tell all, and I don't see how I can 'reveal all' about everyone else and not myself. It would hardly be fair.

The press were picking up on all they could about the blunder, and the television cameras had filmed me at home.

Here we go again, how was I going to face the neighbours? That feeling still existed. When the news article was shown next day on T.V., I seemed so cool, calm, and collected. If only they had known, I was anything but. I had wanted to say certain things but when the cameras started to roll, I would say something completely different. Fortunately, it was still O.K. What I said made sense, I was amazed. How can someone so nervous and terrified of the camera seem so calm, and say all the right things? I couldn't even look at the camera, I was so nervous. I had to keep my eyes on the interviewer. I felt as though I was being driven on by an unseen force. Maybe I was, because the 'drive' is still there.

When walking round to school with Chrissie and Jamie, people seemed to be avoiding me. It was not my imagination. Women who would stop and have a natter with me were walking straight past.

I thought: "Oh heck, how do I deal with this."?

I decided to put a stop to it. If this sounds aggressive, it is not meant to. The first woman I met the next day, one who used to stop and talk, crossed over the street as I approached.

I called over to her, "Hi 'Mary', have I got B.O.?"

She looked over and said, "Oh, Hi Lil, I didn't see you, how are you?" We both knew she did, but the ice was broken, everything was alright again, others started talking to me again. Being straight spoken, or 'hard-faced', which ever you like, I asked them why they had stopped speaking to me. They told me they were afraid of being snubbed. They thought I might have 'gone big-headed after being on the telly'.

I didn't see myself as having changed, and it had not occurred to me that others might.

I was in the public eye almost every day, but I had not become a 'star'. I was leading a campaign. The issue was being publicized because the public had the right to know. It had implications for every woman in Britain. What had happened in Liverpool could just easily have happened anywhere. The cervical screening programme was rubbish.

If the women of Liverpool, the victims, did nothing, then I felt sure that the authorities would have buried the blunder deeply, and quietly. After all, it appeared that the only reason it was publicized, was because of the 'missing

ladies', otherwise, no one would have known. We would have continued to think....
''We are taking better care of you these days'', which is what one doctor told me at the beginning when I asked why I was being recalled earlier than expected.
Then, fate struck a cruel blow!

Chapter 4

DEVASTATION

In the afternoon of June 15th, one of my ‘contacts’ phoned me saying: “I thought I’d better let you know, as the press will be getting in touch with you shortly, Louise was found dead in bed this morning....”

I sat down on my telephone seat with a thump. I felt as though I had received an electric shock. I was stunned. It couldn’t be true, it just couldn’t. I could not *believe* it.

I had spoken to her only two or three days ago, before her operation, and after. She said she was fine.

My contact was shouting down the phone: “Hello, hello, are you there Lily?” This brought me out of my state of shock. I asked for some detail.

I immediately rang Helen, who was also acting for Louise and she confirmed the news.

I was already badly shaken. Now I felt completely done in. This news had effected me more than when I thought that I was going to die.

I had no sooner put the ‘phone down on Helen, when the first reporter rang. Two or three other reporters also rang. They asked for my comments but I was non-commital, saying that we should wait until after the inquest.

The press were not necessarily looking to be sensational. They knew that Louise was one of the recalled ladies. It would therefore seem natural to assume that she may have died of cancer, or as a result of the treatment she had so recently received.

This brought my mind back to the other women. Oh God,

no, they would surely make the same assumptions and panic. I got back to Helen and told her that the press had been in contact, and what they had said. I expressed my concerns about the other women. We decided to hold a meeting in my home, and together we made contact with as many women as possible. Helen rang her clients, and I rang the women who had been in touch with Pat, Pauline and me.

"Tests Death Riddle."

There were many similar headlines, so it was just as well we did act promptly, because women *did* panic and who could blame them. Louise's death had sent shock waves through every woman involved in the mix-up. One newspaper article ended with....

"The inquest was adjourned. No evidence was given of the cause of death."

Helen and I made a radio broadcast, asking that recalled ladies should not panic. We also told them of the meeting which had been arranged.

I was in touch with about sixty of the women, including some of Helen's clients, so if they had all turned up, I don't know where we would have put them. My living room is quite small by comparison to the numbers.

Approximately 28 women came to that first meeting, and a further 20 or so rang to say that they could not attend but would like some information. We explained the facts as we knew them and did our best to comfort those who were openly sobbing, for Louise, a woman we had never met. But we all felt a strange kinship for each other. It was quite weird.

We decided we should put it out of our minds until after the inquest had been resumed. The date for the second hearing was 21st. July.

We arranged to meet every two weeks, on Wednesday evenings. We talked about how we were feeling, any new test we had undergone, and the feeling was good, generally, to get it out in the open. One or two ladies didn't come again because they were frightened by what was being said. The majority thought it was a relief to talk together, and the best thing was the feeling that we were no longer on our own. We were with women who understood because we had all been through it . I think it is fair to say that we all left the meeting feeling better than when we had arrived. Except me of course, because I lived there. We always ended on a light note because laughter has its own way of healing the hurt.

I attended the hearing on July 21st, with Steve Harrison. I stayed pretty much in the background, having no wish to intrude on this family's grief. I needed to know the facts so that I could help the others understand.

"Tragedy of Smear Test Woman."

"Merseyside coroner....made it clear there was no evidence of suicide and recorded a verdict of accidental death."

She did not die as a result of the treatment received or cancer.

I must confess to feeling some relief. Had the verdict been different, I don't know how some of the women would have coped.

Steve and Helen both came to our next group meeting. We told the women about the inquest, and said that it was best to put it out of our minds. Many of the women felt that the cancer blunder had at least played a part in Louise's death by putting extra pressure on her, and certainly I had to agree that she did feel under pressure because she had told me so herself.

We were not suggesting that the coroners verdict was anything other than fair and just, but in a group of 'highly pitched', psychologically damaged women, *fact* played a very small part. We were scared.

This chapter has been kept brief deliberately because Louise's family did not want too much publicity at the time and I certainly will still respect that wish. I did not, however, feel able to omit this epiosde completely, as her passing was instrumental in changing the group from a telephone help-line, to a group which held regular meetings.
I spoke to Louise many times on the telephone, we arranged to meet when she was sufficently recovered. She had a wonderful sparkling personality and it shone through, even on the telephone. Helen did meet her, and agrees with my description.
She called me in her time of need and I shall always remember her. Thoughts of her even now still have the power to bring tears to my eyes. I think of her as a friend. I will end by dedicating this chapter to her memory.

Chapter Five

INTRODUCING POLITICS

If I thought of June as a busy and eventful month, then I don't know how to describe July. It was nerve-racking and highly exciting, not necessarily in a nice way, but it had it's moments.
To me, the blunder was a health issue, the government of the day controlled the health of the nation. The authorities in Liverpool wouldn't take any notice, so I had to go higher. I wouldn't mind, but I hated politics, the only political thing I ever did was vote.
To do justice to this part of my story, I will have to record it in diary style.

July 2nd.

"NEW ROW IN CANCER TEST NIGHTMARE"
"Thousands back bid for public inquiry."
The *Liverpool Daily Post* printed the above in big bold letters. The article dominated the front page, two columns with my photograph at the bottom. I never dreamed that I would share a front page with H.R.H. the Prince of Wales, when he was visiting the 'London Slums'.
"Victims of the massive cancer smear mix-up are demanding a public inquiry into what went wrong."
"Mrs. Hopkins and others are furious.... She will lead a small delegation which will hand over the petition to the health authority...."
"The CHC has written to health minister, John Moore

backing the women's request...."
"Junior health minister, Edwina Currie has promised that the government is keeping a close eye on the situation...."
The women and I had been busy during the last fortnight collecting signatures. We had three thousand or so ready and there were more, but they had not yet been returned. The inquiry panel were ready to reconvene and we wanted to be there on the first day.
We were angry at the many remarks made by those in power who were sitting confortably behind their desks, while we were out in all kinds of weather doing what we thought should have been *their* job, to see that justice was done.
We were so naive, I don't think we even informed the authority of our intentions to present them with a petition. I believe they learned from the press. Mind you, that makes a change, doesn't it!
On the eve of this presentation, several of us were interviewed by the *Liverpool Daily Post*, Steve Harrison of course.
We received double page coverage. In the centre of the page, was a photograph of Steve telling the background story of the blunder. At last we knew the name of the doctor behind the mix-up. Steve really had 'done his homework'.
To the right, was a picture of Maria Partington with the caption, "I couldn't believe I was on the list." She told of terror, tears and nights without sleep. Next, there was the 'other Maria' who talked about her 'Mystery Recall'.
Centre page under Steve was Pauline Barrows who was: "Furious but so worried" and wanted to know "What are they trying to hide?" Pauline had only one kidney, so you can imagine, she had already been through the 'medical hoop'. Now to be told that she may have cancer totally blew her mind.

'Carol' - an assumed name to preserve the lady's identity - was only 27 years old. She had one child and stated: "I don't want my son to be an only child."

She was told that she may have to undergo a hysterectomy. "Staff were very busy. They told me it was like coping with an epidemic."

On the right, was a picture of me with the quote: "There was no counselling, no one to explain to me how to cope."

That quote was the crux of the matter. *They* had made a mistake. *They had called us in for treatment*, and *they* had just dumped us, left us to get on with it.

Did they not realise what it would do to us? Learning from the press that we might have cancer. Why did they not call us in and *talk* to us? Each woman had questions to ask, because it affected us all differently. We were from very different backgrounds, some were working class, some were upper-working class, and some can only be described as 'yuppies'. We had varied levels of intelligence. Some were 'dumb' and some had a higher than average I.Q., yet we were all treated the same, as stupid women who did not have the right to a reasonable explaination. In fact, we were given *no* explanation. The authorities may deny this, but that is how it came across to the women involved, to the media, and to everyone else we spoke to. We can't all be wrong.

Each woman has a different story to tell, about how it affected her and her family, how it changed her life and not for the better. It would take hundreds of pages to tell these stories and perhaps I will another time. It would certainly be 'the Weepy of the Century'. Please do not conclude that we were a bunch of 'weepies'. We were not, we were a group of women desperately trying to get back our health and confidence, and a degree of normality in our lives. We were stopped every step of the way by bureaucracy.

It may seem to the reader that most of my story so far has been made up of press cuttings and media coverage, and this is true, but I would ask you to understand that when the *Daily Post* printed headlines like, "SCARED VICTIMS OF A LIFELINE THAT FAILED", they in fact became our 'lifeline' themselves. We desperately needed someone to listen to what we had to say, and the media provided us with this vital outlet.
We were not used to media coverage and in some ways, we lived for it. Not in the way a pop star might seek publicity, but as a way to vent our pent up feelings. As the 'leader' of the women, I had to learn to handle the press, because mostly, they would approach me first, perhaps asking me to arrange an interview with a particular woman. I had to learn very quickly that some reporters were sensitive and some were not, some wanted to exploit us and some were genuinely concerned. There was even a couple of reporters who offered us money for 'tips' on the more serious cases. None of the women associated with my group ever accepted money for their stories, and neither did I. We were not in it to make money from our own misfortune or from the misfortune of others. We told our stories only so that the public would be kept informed and to enhance our chances of fair play. Other individuals may have been paid for stories, but that was no concern of ours.

July 3rd.
"NO INQUIRY - THATCHER."

"P.M Bars Public Cancer Hearing."
"Mrs. Thatcher rejected calls for an independent inquiry into Liverpool's cervical smear mix-up....despite increasing pressure for a public hearing."
"After learning of the Prime Minister's stance, women

caught up in the error....said they wre now considering taking their 3,000-signature petition to Mrs. Thatcher in person....''
''....was told by Mrs. Thatcher, 'Because there have been mistakes does not mean that one should condemn the the whole system.' ''
One might not condemn the whole system, but *we* did.
O.K., we will accept that 'to err is human.' But 1,000 MISTAKES!!!
No, we would not accept that, not without a reasonable excuse, and we were not being given one.
I wonder whether Mrs. Thatcher would have changed her mind if she were to visit my home when there was a group meeting?
How would she have reacted to the state the women were in, to the tears, fears, and utter misery?
Maybe it would not have bothered her, but it *did* bother me.
I swore to fight to the bitter end, and many would stand by my side.
It was so frustrating and aggravating to see the women like this, while health chiefs sat in their plush offices protecting the guilty party or parties. The is *exactly* what they were doing by keeping us out.
Page three of the same paper carried 'Too scared', Donna Humphries, a young mother of two who had received laser treatment. She said: ''I still can't try for another baby in case they find that it hasn't cleared up and I need further treatment, which might harm the unborn baby.''
Of Mrs. Thatcher's rejection, she said: ''Perhap's if it had happened to Mrs. Thatcher she would be more willing to act.'' Poor Donna, she was in a terrible state emotionally.

Monday, 6th July.

Telephone call from the *Liverpool Daily Post*.
"Steve Harrison speaking.....Did you mean it when you said you would like to take your petition to No 10.?"
"Yes, Steve, I really meant it. The trouble is, I can't afford the fare."
"If you want to go, we will take you at our expense."
Well, I jumped in and readily accepted. This is what had kept us back, lack of cash.
It was arranged for a car to call for me to meet Steve at the station.
Next morning, I had multiple butterflies in my tummy. Would Mrs. Thatcher be there? What would I say to her if she was? How should I treat her? How would she receive me?
I decided that although she was the country's leading lady, she was still a human being. Some people had their doubts about that, but I was not politically prejudiced. I took people as I found them. She had the power to sort this mess out. She could order a public inquiry, if I could persuade her that it was the right thing to do.
We arrived in London and took a taxi to Downing Street. The newspaper had arranged for us to get through the barrier. I hadn't thought about getting permission to go through, but the security police were expecting us and let us go straight to the door, the famous number ten. I didn't really believe that this was happening. What was I doing outside number 10 Downing Street. I must be dreaming.
The door was opened by a uniformed gentleman. He said that the Prime Minister was up-stairs having tea. He would see she received the petition.
The Leading Lady could not even be bothered to come out to meet her 'subjects'. Maybe she didn't want to give us more publicity. Some of the women thought she was afraid, but most thought that she was just not interested in a

woman from Liverpool. It is thought not to be Mrs. Thatcher favourite city, whatever the reason. I handed the petition to the gentleman, accompanied by a letter.
Steve had made arrangements for me to visit the House of Commons to meet with my constituency M.P. Mr. Bob Wareing.
When we arrived, he was not yet available. Mr. Frank Field offered to show us round until Mr. Wareing came in. It felt strange, being in this building where so much of our history had been made. I even witnessed a ceremony which reflected the pomp and pageantry of our British heritage. I'm not too sure exactly what it was, I was much to busy looking around, trying to take everything in. I love history.
We were out on the terrace having coffee when Bob Wareing arrived. Steve asked about the possiblity of me meeting Edwina Currie, the Junior health minister. A telephone call later told us that Mrs. Currie was engaged at a previous meeing and could not see us.
We were again having refreshments on the terrace when a further telephone call explained that Mrs Currie's meeting had been cancelled. She would see us after all.
We finished our tea and the two M.P.'s led us through a maze of passages to Mrs. Currie's office. After introductions, the minister said that we would be more comfortable on the balcony as her office was rather small. Back home in Liverpool, we would have described it as, 'not enough room to swing a cat'.
As we made our way through the cobbled yard, Mrs. Currie and I, followed by the two M.P.'s, then Steve Harrison, and a photographer. Mrs. Currie reminded me that Liverpool was her home town. Perhaps it was strange to her that I also claimed Liverpool as *my* home town, complete with my Scottish accent. At least I didn't have a 'plum in my mouth'. I had lived in the city for thirty years at that time,

so I think one could say that my claim was legitimate.
Anyway, I hadn't come to London to argue about who was scouse and who was not. She went on to speak about people from Liverpool liking too many chips. Chips? What had they got to do with it. Perhaps she was trying to make me feel at home. I answered that I didn't like chips but ate cabbage with my meals. She asked how did I like my cabbage? I replied: "with a knob of butter". Neither of us were trying to be smart, I don't think, it was just light, but leading banter.
We reached the balcony and Mrs. Currie and I ordered fresh orange juice. While she was away, Bob Wareing remarked: "She looks so damned healthy", and she did. Her eyes were bright and alert and she was a fine figure of a woman. I am tempted to add...."for her age" but I won't.
We discussed the blunder for a time and Mrs. Currie said she was having dinner that evening with Mr. Fitzpatrick, chair of the L.H.A., and she would see what she could do about setting up a meeting for me.
Of course, she brought up the subject of me smoking. (I wasn't smoking at that moment,) and advised me to stop. I said it was not the right time to stop smoking, with all the additional pressure from the mix-up, but agreed that it might not be such a good thing to smoke, but also added that I didn't necessarily believe that smoking caused cervical cancer, (thinking to myself, I don't smoke in my cervix). Childish? Well maybe so!
The meeting came to an end with Mrs. Currie saying that she thought our request for a public inquiry was premature, and suggested we wait until the internal review published its report. Fair enough, we'll wait and see.
Steve brought me fish and chips in the snack bar in Euston station while we were waiting for our train home.
We got to know each other a bit better. He was a very

intense young man, but you couldn't help liking him. He was a cracker. He showed such interest in the person he was interviewing. He really captured the art of reporting.
Back home, the women couldn't wait to hear what I had to say about Edwina Currie. She isn't the most popular woman on Merseyside. There was a group meeting arranged for the following evening, but some of the women couldn't wait for this and telephoned me for news. As you can imagine, there was a lot of wise-cracking about Edwina, smoking and chips. I was glad I had met Mrs. Currie, it took the women's minds off their problems for a while, and we could laugh, and how!

Chapter 6

DIARY OF JULY

July, 7th.

Front page coverage. Photograph of yours truly outside number 10, with the heading: "LILY TAKES IT TO THE TOP."
"Mrs. Hopkins hands in her petition at number Ten Downing Street."
The article mentioned I had a face to face meeting with Edwina Currie and that we had spoken for more than an hour.
It went on to say that "about 30 victims were now taking legal advice.", and quoted me as saying: "Now that this issue has been brought to the attention of a Minister, I hope it receives the attention it deserves." Also stated was the fact that Mrs. Currie would be 'grilled' by M.P.'s over the mix-up and subsequent inquiry during a debate tonight in the Commons.
That debate did take place, and Mrs. Currie sent me a transcript of it.
Edwina Currie kept to her word. She did arrange a meeting with the Chairman of the L.H.A.
My impressions of her were that she had taken an interest, she had helped in what ways she could, but I don't think she had enough power to do more. That part was up to the Prime Minister, or another senior Minister. I therefore feel that it would be unfair to blame her for not doing more. She did what she could. Unfortunately, it was not enough to

satisfy us. We would however wait until the internal review published the report.

July, 8th.

Radio Merseyside had arranged to send a reporter, Sue Polhill, along to our group meeting to interview some of the women.
She used a portable cassette recorder. We were all rather nervous. I suppose that added to the impact, because you could tell how we felt when the tape was played back.
Can you imagine all the ooh's and ah's, and "thats not *my* voice,"...."I didn't say *that*?" "Oh no, don't I sound terrible?"
We had a good laugh about the remarks made, including Sue. She was great, just like one of us. I can't thing of anything worse than listening to your own voice on tape, during a serious conversation. I hated the sound of my voice, it sounded so deep, almost like a mans. Pity I hadn't been a man. I wouldn't have had all these problems.
It may sound to the reader, that we did more laughing than crying, but that wasn't so. All these little interludes were what helped to keep us going. If it had all been crying and moaning, we would have cracked up. Anyone who has been through a similar situation will understand, We had to keep our spirits high because we had a long way to go, and God knows, it wasn't easy. Some of us were to undergo further treatment, and most of us hadn't yet been cleared. These were early days.

July, 9th.

My introduction to Radio City and Johnnie Kennedy. He rang me on the morning of the 9th, and asked if I was

prepared to do a 'telephone interview' for his programme. I said I was, and he went through what he wanted to ask me.
Johnny had seen the morning papers about my visit to the Commons and my talk with Edwina Currie. He wanted to know how she felt about the mix-up. He led into the programme by explaining, for the benefit of his listeners, what had happened in Liverpool. I told of the conversation between Mrs. Currie and me, and added that I had no direct contact with the authority of Mr. Fitzpatrick. Johnny said that *Radio City* had spoken with Mr. Fitzaptrick who was sympathetic but stated that he must remain impartial. I said we wanted only to discuss our health care and that we needed certain reassurances. Johnny brought men into the conversation saying that they weren't 'clued up' on how women feel about 'this sort of thing' and asked me to tell of our feelings. The interview continued by mentioning the 'missing ladies'.
The 'missing ladies' were a number of women who had been contracted by the Health Authorities, but had not responded to the letter.
I explained to Johnny that I was unsure as to the number of ladies who had not responded, and stated that the authority had, not surprisingly, been 'cagey' about giving out numbers. I believed there were between 38, and 58 ladies involved.
I made a plea to these ladies to come forward to be tested. I was very worried because some of them might have been walking round with cancer, and not be aware of it. Some of them could die.
To me, the authority was not doing enough to find these women, so it seemed sensible for me to try to help. I gave listeners the number of the Women's Hospital, and my own number, saying that all women who were tested between March 1983 and December 1985, should 'ring and check'

just to be on the safe side, and to give themselves peace of mind.
Once again, there was chaos at home, the phone rang almost non-stop. Mostly from women who were too scared to ring the hospital themselves, in case their name *was* on the list. Such was the fear among the general public.
Apparently, the phones at the hospital were jam-packed for hours. This didn't exactly please the authority. They issued a press statement to the effect that "Mrs. Hopkins is well-intentioned and has the women's best interests at heart," but went on say that my broadcast had "not been helpful".
Oh, dear, it seems that I got up their nose. I must be honest and say that I was more concerned with finding the missing women than the feelings of the authority. If only one lady came forward, then it was worth it. I never did find out whether any did. They were not likely to tell me.
I collected quite a long list of ladies who were worried that their name might be on the list, but were afraid to ring themselves, and I decided to ring the hospital cytology department to ask if they would check my list.
The woman at the cytology department was very nice. She told me there had been a good response to my broadcast. I apologised for giving her so much extra work and explained my reasons. She agreed that my efforts *had* created extra work, but said it would be worth it if some of the missing ladies were to ring. She was quite happy to check my list, which was all clear, but I was able to help some of the callers with other problems so my efforts were not in vain.
The *Daily Post* continued our 'saga' mainly covering my meeting with Mrs. Currie in more detail and carrying headlines......
"THE CANCER CASE SCANDAL .....ONE WOMAN'S BATTLE."

"Key inquiry stays private."
"Grandma Lily pledges fight to the end."
I could have killed Steve for the 'Grandma' quip. I *was* a Grannie of course, but what did that have to do with it? Only joking, Steve!
At the bottom of the page, and on a more serious note, a picture of little
Pat Kirwan. She had been refused legal aid.
"FEARS FOR COMPENSATION."
"Legal setback for Pat."
Pat is quoted as saying: "I am disgusted, shocked and devastated...the only way I can pay, is to save up."
Pat really crumbled when she heard that news. Her bottom lip was trembling and she was close to tears. She would appeal, of course, but it made us feel very small, that we had to fight for what most people believe to be their basic right, to fight for justice.
The problem was, you see, not to prove that the blunder had occurred but to prove that we had suffered as a result. How do you prove your pain and mental stress? No one else can feel that pain, so how on earth are you supposed to prove it in the legal sense?
We needed expert opinions, meaning that we had to engage Consultant Gyneacologists, Pathologists, and Psychologists to prepare reports, which cost money. That is what we were lacking, *hard cash*!
They had committed a massive error, and now the Law Society were insulting us further by saying that we had not suffered enough to quantify at least £500.00. in damages. Worse still, we were not even being given the opportunity to state our cases. Just how did they justify that?
We were fuming. We would certainly appeal. We were not prepared to take this lying down.

Max Marcus, who was Pat's solicitor, said: "All cases are supposed to be decided individually, but if they are taking that sort of attitude on this type of case, it will act as an effective precedent."

In the beginning, when the authority was asked to make an offer of compensation, they said that each case had to be judged on its own merit, but now, by refusing up to 14 clients legal aid, they were surely going back on that. We were either a 'block', or we were not. They couldn't have it have both ways. We would fight on.

Max, of course, was quite right. If they persisted with this type of action, then the first case to reach the courts, would become a 'test case'.

On the same page...."CURRIE'S PLEA OVER TEST CHECKS."

There were still 50 women missing.

Max ended 'Pat's story' by saying: "They can't say that compensation is likely to be less than £500. Because they have not seen the medical reports."

July, 10th.

I received a reply from Mrs. Thatcher's private secretary saying that the Prime Minister had received my letter, together with my petition, and this was receiving attention. A reply would be sent as soon as possible.

I did my very first television interview with B.B.C. You may remember I mentioned T.V. appearances earlier on, but this was on a one-to-one basis. It was quite different from just having the camera's around, like during our demonstration. It was rather scary. Winifred Robinson, the interviewer, was a very experienced lady. She very quickly put me at ease. She said not to worry if I made a mistake, that they would cut it out. It certainly helped to know that.

I believe this was the first time I said that we had been "treated like stupid housewives". When the piece was screened, I looked very confident. Boy, I wish I'd felt the way I looked.
That weekend, I spent replying to letters I had received from worried ladies who had heard me on the radio. Also, preparing for our presentation of signatures to the Health Authority on Monday.

July, 13th.

When I arrived at the LHA headquarters in Myrtle Street, Pat, Marie, and Donna from our group were already there.
So were the T.V. people, the radio and the press.
I had seen Mr. Fitzpatrick, the chair, on television and he looked to me to be a short, stout gentleman. I led the women into the building to be greeted by the Chairman and the Administrator, a Mr. Criddle, and to receive my first shock of the morning.
Mr. Fitzaptrick stepped forward to shake my hand. I looked at him up and up. He was a very tall and slim man, nothing like I had imagined. He accpeted my petition saying that if I would like to come along to the review, I could make a statement. I would be very welcome. That was shock number two.
Television camera's came closer, flash bulbs flashed, and there were microphones everywhere.
I had no speech prepared. How could I, I was not told in advance. I saw this move as intimidation tactics. Maybe I'm wrong, I don't know, but I am entitled to my opinion. Anyway, I couldn't stand dithering, I had to make my mind up fast. Was I going to be able to speak to the review. More importantly, would I be able to make sense of it without due consideration? I did not feel I had a choice. If I refused,

they would say that I had my chance. No, I had no choice, I had to speak.

I accepted the offer saying I would be delighted to speak to the review.

I was walking alone, chatting with Mr. Fitzpatrick, so intensely, I did not notice that the other women had been escorted into a taxi to take them to the review. We reached his car, and he held the door open for me. I am not too sure whether or not I should have been in his car. I was so busy talking I didn't think. I just automatically stepped in. We were talking about doctors' attitudes to their patients. I said it appeared that when doctors reached consultancy level, they forgot how to talk to patients. Even when they did try, it sometimes came across as patronage.

Mr. Fitzpatrick agreed, saying it was not only doctors who forgot, but others who had climbed the ladder. I don't suppose these were his exact words, but the meaning is the same.

We reached the Royal Liverpool Hospital, where the review was being held. I was re-joined by the other ladies. We were all shown into a boardroom, where the panel which was made up of four people, and others were present. I did not know at that moment, who the 'others' were, but apparently they were witnesses and their legal representatives. The atmosphere was somewhat 'court-room' in appearance, with the panel seated at the top, and the 'others', at both sides. I was shown to a table in the middle of the floor. Mr. Fitzpatrick said that I could now make my statement. I could not ask questions nor could I be questioned.

I was unsure as to what I should say, and decided I would best to tell the panel just what we were looking for in their report. I said we were not necessarily looking for "heads to roll". We were more interested in finding out how it

happened, and what was going to be done to ensure that it didn't happen again. I can't remember my exact workds but I believe I spoke for about ten minutes.
The press were waiting to interview me after I had spoken, and I explained to them that we were now prepared to wait until the review published their report before deciding about a public inquiry, saying that if we got the answers we were looking for, we would not press for a public inquiry.
This was the last day the review would be meeting until September so we had a few weeks to wait.
That evening, I attended a Health and Education meeting. This was part of my 'learning process.' I had such a lot to learn about everything, and meetings were a very good place to learn. Books were great, but you can't learn everything out of them. There is no substitute for practical experience and speaking to people.
Later, the women and I had a discussion about the review 'speech'. They said I did O.K. I wasn't too sure about this, but supposed that under the circumstances, I had done the best I could. We felt better that at least, we had made ourselves heard. Whether *they* listened or not, was another matter. We would know soon enough.

July, 14th.

This morning I received a letter from Edwina Currie's private secretary with a copy of the script of the parliamentary debate. This would promote discussion for my women's group meeting next week.
Although I am not politically minded, I found the dialogue interesting. I was faintly amused to find that a parliamentary debate was made up of a 'play on words'. This was something I am quite good at myself, maybe I should have been a politician. Makes me sound very

cynical. Really I'm not, it's just that being raw to the methods used by 'higher authority'. I was just not used to it. I soon discovered that doctors, like lawyers, like politicians, all had their own brand of 'play-on-words' method to get their point across without offending their colleagues. In fact, I was to use that very same method in years to come, but I didn't know that then. I learned a lot from those people.

July, 15th.

"PRIVATE EYES TRY TO FIND CANCER WOMEN."
"The man in charge of the operation, hospital manager Pearse Butler, said the decision to employ private detectives was an extreme step but justifiable."
"Despite a three-month search...the authority has failed to make contact with 17 women."
Now we knew how many women were still missing. They had to search all over the world, and yet they were playing the matter down at home.
They were saying that the women they were looking for would be women who had changed their names or addresses or G.P.'s.
They were also saying that if a women failed to respond, they were sending a health visitor to knock on doors. The last part was true. They sent someone to knock on *my* door, and yet I hadn't changed my name, or my address, or my G.P. I had responded immediately to their letter. This left we wondering if they knew what they were doing in any sense of the word.
Several of the women were in exactly the same position as me. They had not changed their address, doctor or name, etc. The sheer panic of the authority did not match what they were saying to us - don't worry. How could we not worry

with all this going on? They were botching the whole thing and, at the same time, expecting us to have confidence in them. Were they for real? We were more mis-trusting than ever.
I had an appointment to meet with Mr. Fitzpatrick that very day. I tried to make him see how we felt and why. He was very symapthetic to our feelings, but tried to encourage us to wait for the report. We didn't really have a choice about that, and I told him so. I was more concerned about the women who had been traced and ensuring that they were being treated adequately and sensitively. We had quite a long discussion. I found him a proper gentleman and a very likeable person. I felt sure he had his own opinion of what was happening but he kept it to himself, which was fair enough, because I certainly wasn't confiding in him, however nice he was. He was still one of *them*.

***July, 16th*.**

I spent the early part of the day answering telephone calls and studying. Quite a number of women were contacting me now. Some were not involved with the mix-up but just felt lost. Some wondered if they were involved and had not been told, because you see, there was a wide discrepancy in the figures given out by the authority.
Firstly, we were told 487 women were involved, then 911. This was quite puzzling, and worrying for all the women who had a smear test taken at the time. *We* didn't know what laboratory our smears were sent to, and of course, it was only smears which had been analysed at the Women's Hospital which were in dispute. Instead of the authority issuing a very clear directive to the public, they were issuing bits and pieces. Every woman in Liverpool was worried. They, who had accused me of 'panicking' people,

were doing a much better job than me, by with-holding information.
In the evening, I took time off to attend the AGM in my son's school. I tried very hard not to lose sight of my family. It was not easy. My whole concept of family life had to be changed. I had to 'fit in' with events and publications. I would have to become more organised. Mind you, I thought, it will all be over by the end of the year. I did not envisage it going on for more than four years. Where would it end?

July, 17th.

I made my first 'home visit'. This was 'one of us'.
She was so bad that a relative phoned to ask if I could help. I was more than willing to help, but was a little afraid of what I would find. What did the relative mean by 'bad'. Was it her health? Did she have invasive cancer? or was it an emotional/nervous problem? No matter, I would do what I could. If it was beyond my scope, I would alert the authority and get them to do something for her.
It broke my heart to see this young woman sitting up in her bed. I was not prepared for the sight which met me. She looked, for all the world, like a person suffering bad withdrawal symptoms. She was shivering and shaking and her eyes were red from crying. I went over and sat on the end of her bed.
She caught hold of my hand: "Please tell me I haven't got cancer."
She again started to weep.
I tried to calm her down a bit, I asked her relative to bring us some tea. We drank the tea and had a smoke. You might think that smoking wasn't such a good idea, but I can

tell you, in our state, it's a wonder we didn't resort to something worse than cigarettes.
Eventually I made sense of her story. She had not been recalled, she was one of the women I named 'the remainder'. You will remember I said about the discrepancy in figures. Well it appears that the laboratory staff, after finding out that the consultant in charge seemed to be taking no notice of their concerns, started their own 'recall system' and succeeded in bringing in, for treatment, some 424 women. Many statements had been made about these women, but the authority would not confirm them. This caused a lot of worry. A number of women who had been back for treatment, were left wondering if they were part of the mix-up. This young lady seemed to fit into this catagory. I was able to re-assure her by looking at hospital cards and various letters she had received. It appeared she had been treated a year ago. She might feel better if she had a chat with her G.P. and maybe ask for a smear to be taken for her own peace of mind.
I describe this girl's case in detail so that the reader may understand the distress caused by this 'mix-up'. This was to be the first of many such visits.

July, 20th

I went to Broughton Hall High School's production of 'Annie', because my daughter, Julie had made the costumes so I couldn't miss it. This was my first real break since the campaign began, and I really enjoyed it. The 'artistes' were all under 16. They put on a marvellous performance, and Julie had 'done them proud' with the costumes. The hall was packed with parents and relatives. The atmosphere was great. It certainly took my mind off the problem. Just what I needed to start afresh next day. Julie's name was on the programme as 'wardrobe mistress'. I have kept the programme, of course.

July 21st

What a day! You may remember that I attended Louise's inquest in the morning, then I had a date to speak at the Womens Labour Movement at 7.00p.m. Also my son was having his school concert at 6.30. Now this was impossible. I couldn't be in two places at once. What was I going to do? If only I had been told the date of the school concert earlier, I would not have agreed to speak at the meeting. I couldn't let them down. Chris and Liz would have to attend the concert, Jamie would be disappointed, but I would promise to come to his Christmas play.

The WLM, naturally, being women, wanted to know what had happened and how it had effected the women involved. They were to become very supportive to us, as did most womens groups. They helped us raise funds, and to pass out our literature, but I'll mention more of that later on.

Our story had now reached the national papers, with headlines: "CAN CONFIDENCE BE RESTORED IN SMEAR TESTING?"

"The issues raised by the medical blunder in Liverpool."

I had been interviewed at some length by the *Daily Telegraph.* They covered much the same ground as the local papers, but added the 'sex-life' angle. Many people, I suppose, wanted to avoid talking about this very personal aspect, but I knew just how badly the others were affected. I decided that it had to be said. It was an important part of our lives and it had virtually been taken away from us.

The paper handled it very sensitively, quoting me: "There's no physical reason why we should not make love. It's all in the mind. If you had a cancerous sore on your hand you would not shake hands with anybody." That statement was general one, it did not relate to me, personally. I had not been cleared and so I would not have dreamed of making love. But some of the others had been cleared and they no more could think of lovemaking than I. They also up-dated the number of hysterectomies, which now stood at six. A far cry from the authorities' "no one needs major surgery" of the early days. See what I mean about *them* playing down the situation..

Peter Pallot, the reporter, covered the issue very thoroughly. He wrote: "In the light of the Liverpool fiasco it is not fanciful to suppose that women elsewhere who have been regularly screened but have been diagnosed as suffering from cancer might demand to see an earlier smear, opening up the possiblity of litigation if an expert could attest that it showed pre-cancerous evidence."

This is exactly what women outside the mix-up thought. This was indeed their worry. "What if they got it wrong in my case also?"

A lady called Jan Gauntlett, who was a laboratory manager had written to Edwina Currie, urging a licensing system for all laboratories, backed by examinations for staff. She stated that many cytologists received training only on the job. Now this may sound like the perfect excuse for what happened in Liverpool, but, not so, as you will discover later.

The article was concluded by a statement from Mr. Fitzpatrick: "I'm sorry we had to go behind closed doors for this inquiry, but it did mean that we could take the evidence clearly and accurately and I hope we will be able to draw conclusions."

Really, what he was saying in that statement, was that *he* did not object to an open inquiry, but the witnesses did. Now what could we make of that, other than that they had something to hide. That statement endorsed our feelings.

July, 22nd.

The early part of this day was taken up with a telephone interview with the *Daily Mirror*, and a few calls from the women.
In the evening, I had to go to little Chrissie's school for a parents' meeting. I then had to rush home for our fortnightly group meeting. We had a lot to discuss. First, the parliamentary debate, then the article in the *Daily Telegraph* and Jan Gauntlett's offering.
It was obvious that the whole system for testing smears was a shambles, but it wasn't to blame for the Liverpool incident. From what we had learned so far, it seemed that it was not the laboratory staff who were to blame. It had even been suggested it was the fault of the consultant in charge. Again, we would have to wait for the report. Our life at that time was made up of waiting. Waiting for results, treatment, to be cleared, and now the report. Some of our frustrations came out on the family life. We were beginning to feel the full effects of the blunder.
Each time we met it seemed that at least one had visibly aged. We looked tired and drawn. We *felt* that way too. The group meetings became our refuge, we could let it all out. Sometimes the language was choice, but no one took offence as we understood each others different needs. Chris, was the 'tea-boy' and my girls were the waitresses, passing in endless cups of tea.
Yes, I think it would be true to say that most people left the group meeting feeling better than when they had come. It

also helped me personally, to think that I was helping others. We all got something out of it. It was expensive for little Pat, because of her worsening agoraphobia. She had to commute by taxi, all the way from Speke to Fazakerley, which was quite an expense. Pauline too, felt the cost, and a few others. I didn't have travelling expenses, but I provided the tea, coffee, and when I was flush, a few 'biccies'. No one was thinking about money. This was something we had to do. If there was enough women from the same area, they could share, but this wasn't always the case. Still, we managed.

Thursday and Friday were spent answering telephone calls which had come in when I was out. I didn't like to leave these calls longer than a day or two, in case it was someone in real distress. I didn't dare to think about my telephone bill. Prior to the blunder it had been very low, maybe about £1 or £2 per week.

Now?

July 25th.

A woman called Sue Quilliam called on me at home. The meeting had been pre-arranged. Sue was writing a book on positive smears, having had one herself. She was travelling around the country, getting the opinion of other women, and high-lighting the problems. I was very pleased that someone was doing something. I readily gave her the information she requested. Little did I know, that one day I would also write a book, although, I must say, I would still have given her the information. The public had the right to different people's opinions. I have read many books myself on the same subject and every author makes a different point. Sue said she would let me know when the book was being published as, naturally, I wanted to read the finished work.

She later invited me to attend the launch of her book in London, and asked me to take part in a workshop about abnormal smears.

B.B.C. television had been back in touch and asked me to arrange a 'group interview' with them. This would take place on Monday.

July, 27th.

I was sitting in the hall talking to a lady on the telephone when I heard the post box rattling. I looked over to the front door, and saw the flap being lifted and a letter gingerly put through. I remarked to my caller. I think it was Pauline: "I hope it's not a letter-bomb," the way it was put through the letterbox so carefully. The letter had my name on the front and at the bottom, in bold lettering: *Prime Minister.* At the back of the envelope was *10 Downing Street.* The poor postman! Whatever must he have thought?
The letter was typed but Mrs. Thatcher had handwritten my name and her signature at the end. It began........

"Dear Mrs. Hopkins,
Thank you for your letter of 7th July and the accompanying petition expressing concern about cervical smear tests carried out .. .and seeking a public inquiry."
And ended ....''I'm sorry this may seem a disappointing response to your petition but I hope it helps to clarify the position.''
It was exactly the response we expected. Nevertheless, there was a 'glimmer of hope' that perhaps the Prime Minister would reconsider. Perhaps she, our 'leading lady' would be sympathetic to our plight. We would certainly have

expected this sort of response from a male Prime Minister, but not from a woman. Oh well, back to the drawing board. Tuesday and Wednesday were spent at home working on Liz's wedding dress, and trying to catch up on my housework which had been badly neglected. The girls did their best, but like a lot of mothers, I had my own way of working.

July, 30th.

Helen had noticed I was going downhill and suggested that I ease up a little. I explained to her that it was not the work load but the worry over the next operation. I was in a lot of pain at this time, unexplained pain. I might add, my back hurt, and I had quite severe pelvic pains. Period pains were beyond description. This was all new to me. I had never suffered from period pains. I was sure that the cancer had spread. The work load, in fact, helped take my mind off my problems.
Helen took me to lunch and we talked about all sorts of things. She, trying to lead me away from the problem, and me, leading her right back. My appetite was very poor. I picked at food, having no real inclination to eat. I was beginning to look haggard. I, who at one time would not go out without my make-up, was starting to neglect my appearance. I looked tidy enough, but not the way I used to look.
Later that day, I attended another meeting to talk about the blunder. So July had gone. What a busy little month it was. My diary for August was much less demanding.
I looked to August with apprehension. We had the wedding, which would be the highlight of the month, but I had also been booked in to have my second operation.
I was not looking forward to that.

Chapter 7

MY FAMILY

August came in gently enough. Chris had to go on a Restart interview, and I had a group meeting on the fifth.
Most of the weekend I had spent on Liz's wedding dress which was now complete except for the trimmings, and as any dressmaker will know, they take longer than the actual making.
It was coming along nicely and I was beginning to feel the excitement. The maids' dresses were almost finished, thanks to Julie's help. Church arrangements were more or less complete, only the catering to do. We were still sorting out our lists, but I had the basic menu prepared. 'Course, there was the usual, "if you invite her, you'll have to invite him"...."if they come you'll have to ask the others," and so our list grew. We managed to edit the lists, and it was now a case of "Oh, I wish we had hired a hall for the afternoon as well as the night." The numbers had seemed small and we had decided to have the early reception at home as money was a bit tight. My brothers had chipped in with a few quid to help out. Anyway, it was not too late to think about a hall, so we would just have to manage. If it was a nice day, we could always throw them out in the garden, which was not so badly neglected in those days. The garden had been my 'domain'. Now it was left to Chris because I just didn't have the time. Chris, in my garden? Chris, who had once mowed down my lovely peas with the lawnmower. Oh no! Sorry, Chris, you don't have 'green fingers' but you do keep it tidy.

My cousin John, who lived in Glasgow, was getting married on the 6th August. I would have loved to go,,but there was no way. I wasn't so very well. Also, I had so much to do with Liz's wedding and our legal aid appeal. I was really upset at not being able to go. I had missed my favourite cousin Gini's wedding as well. When Gini got married, I was recovering from the caeserian birth of little Chrissie. I sent cards of course. Gini, if you are reading this, do you remember the 'Jelly Baby card'? This was a reminder of our youth. When Gini and I were teenagers, we used to go to the cinema with large bags of Jelly Babies and Jelly beans, where we proceeded to 'throw them at the boys' for a laugh. This might seem like a harmless bit of fun unless you happened to have caught a jelly baby in your lovely beehive hairdo, or unless you were a young man wearing a nice new Italian suit and you sat on one. Oh well, the folly of youth.

On Monday, August 10th, I was again speaking at a meeting of the Womens Labour Council. They wanted an up-date on the legal aid issue. Like most people, they were appalled at the refusal of legal aid to our recall women. Although I was still apolitical and intended to remain so, I have got to give credit where it is due. The Womens Labour Movement helped us tremendously. They circulated leaflets and news items of our endeavours, and also collected some money to help our legal aid problem. While it would have been impossible to raise enough money to pay for everyone's case to proceed, we certainly managed to help quite a few. This, of course came later. Certain solicitors had made appeals on behalf of their own clients and again, we were playing the waiting game.

There were, I believe, three main political parties during 1987, and we received varying degrees of help from all, as you will see as the story unfolds. It is difficult to mention politics and yet not become involved, but that is what I managed to do. I made it quite clear to all concerned that I was not a member of any political party and who I voted for on polling days was my private business. I was not being un-polite, nor was I being ungrateful, but I was determined not to be known as just a member of the opposition This was a health issue and that is the way it was going to stay. Our ladies were of differing political opinions, but but that did not mean we were not still incensed by the blunder or that we didn't want it made public, because we did, every one of us.

I must mention our feelings here, as we have become aware that the authorities in Liverpool could not, or would not resolve the matter to our satisfaction. It was therefore up to the government of the day to do something, no matter who they might be.

Next day I had a dental appointment, and on the 12th, a meeting had been arranged for me with Dr. June Philips, the MOH for Liverpool. This was the outcome of my meeting with Mr. Fitzpatrick in July. I had said that there were not very many leaflets on the smear test etc., and thought that I might like to write one myself. Dr. Philips agreed that it may be possible, depending on what I "came up with". At the end of the day, it was not necessary for me to write a leaflet, as there were quite a lot about on this subject. They were just not accessible. I began to collect leaflets for distribution to my ladies. I was amazed at how many there were, and yet in all the years I had been going for smears, I had never seen one. None of the others had seen leaflets and this was because apparently you 'had to ask' for them. How ridiculous, hundreds of leaflets had been printed and then placed in a cupboard until someone had a 'brainwave' and actually asked for one. Who is likely to ask for leaflets that you don't know exist?

I had written to the Chairman to ask if I could have a copy of the Internal Review Report prior to the press conference which had been arranged, stating that I wished to peruse the document before being questioned by the press about it's contents. I felt this was only fair to the women, and to the Health Authority. I truly wanted to be fair to all concerned. How could I be expected to answer the many questions which I was sure would be asked if I received the report at the press conference? The authority did not seem to think this a problem because they refused my request in a letter from Administration dated 14th, August 1987.

Oh well, I'll just have to 'play it by ear'. They could hardly accuse me of saying the wrong thing, having refused what I thought was a resaonable request.

A lot of articles on cervical screening began to appear in women's magazines and newspapers, some with good advice and some medicocre. It didn't matter what kind of advice was being given provided it wasn't bad of course, because it brought to the attention of women everywhere the importance of being screened. One Sunday newspaper even funded their own mobile screening unit. This was great, we could be doing with more if this. Women's groups were popping up all over the place. Although some only lasted a short time because they couldn't get any funding, I felt it still helped. I didn't think of applying for funding because, as I said before, I thought our group would break up as soon as the recall women had their case and health settled.

I wasn't so very busy during the remainder of August. I had kept it pretty well clear. Apart from my own group meeting and Jamie's dental appointment, I wanted to rest a bit ready for my next op.

The wedding dress was finished, so were the two main bridesmaids'. Little Chrissie and Cheryl-Ann, my future

son-in-law's little girl from his previous marriage, were going to be 'little maids'. They would look lovely in the white and peach dresses with 'sticky-out skirts'.
Friday, 14th, nothing to do but get ready for Liz's hen-night on Saturday. I was really looking forward to that.
The girls and I decided that, as I was Scottish born, we would follow the the good old Scottish tradition of 'dressing up the bride' for her hen night. This was great fun. Liz was going mad. We dressed her up in a long net curtain with a pair of lace knickers and 'sussies' pinned on to her skirt. We also hung notices on her back, for example, 'I've booked the church and the hall, I've got the ring, all I need is the man!' and, 'If you fancy me, you better do something about it, this is your last chance!'. You should have seen Liz's face! We were to meet Auntie Celina in a pub in Kirkdale, and from there, we marched Liz down the Scottie Road, and before we headed for town to meet the 'future out-laws', we jammed her in the revolving doors of a pub called 'One flew over the Cookoo's Nest'. What a laugh, not for Liz maybe, but for everyone else. I think it is true to say that we girls had a much better time than the men who went out with Chuck for his bachelor night. The men had hired a kissogram in the form of a policewoman with balloons. We went one better and had the real McCoy. Three lovely policemen from St Annes St station kindly 'arrested' Liz and carried her back to the police car for photographs. One of them was so good looking, she was tempted to dump Chuck and marry him instead.
During the time we were waiting for a Internal Review to publish their report, the press kept a pretty low profile. Some articles however did appear, such as "BACKLOG OF TESTS", "Cervical Cancer Delay, Edwina replies."
It was becoming clear that other laboratories were also having problems with smear test reporting. Women all over

Britain were being kept waiting up to twelve weeks for their results, longer if they required treatment. In Liverpool, *they* had an excuse because, in order to discover the extent of the blunder, they had to check through 45,000 smears. What was the excuse in other labs? The screening system was falling to bits all around us. Laboratories were underfunded and understaffed. In some places, the staff themselves were standing up to say this.

Edwina Currie was making statements like: "85% of women who die from cervical cancer have never had a smear test.", ..."We have put £50 million pounds into the system"...." A positive result does not mean that the woman has cancer". This must have been a great consolation to women who had an abnormal smear, and who were waiting for treatment. They wanted treatment *now*! They did not want to wait until it had grown into cancer. That was the object of the exercise, to prevent the abnormalities from progressing to true cancer.

Mrs. Currie had a reputation for putting her foot in it, and she did this extremely well during a television broadcast when she addressed my name.

She said, "I have heard what Mrs. Hopkins, the lady from Liverpool, has said, and I have met her. I suggest to Mrs. Hopkins that if she had never had a smear, she would not have been picked up and treated."

Now, how was that for cheek? I was supposed to be grateful for being picked up and made a mess of! I followed government recommendations, went for regular smears so I should have been treated as soon it became evident that something was wrong. My smear test should have been correctly assessed not 'missed'. But no, according to Mrs. Currie, I should have been happy that *they* had bungled it. At a later date, Mrs. Currie was invited to appear on a television show with me to discuss the issue. She declined.

That surely speaks for itself.
I put myself in the hands of the operators of the system. The least I should be able to expect, is that *they* do their job properly. I did not expect miracles.
Saturday, 22nd August dawned with dark clouds in the sky. Oh no, not rain on Liz's wedding day. It had poured down early that morning and we were praying it would stay off until after the actual ceremony. As the morning wore on, the sun came peeking out at intervals. We were bustling around getting ready. Time to go. Liz was a bundle of nerves. She looked beautiful, a dream bride. We took lots of photographs of her leaving the house on Chris's arm. He looked good as well, but I didn't tell him.
The Good Shephard Church in Croxteth is a lovely church, and the vicar delivered a wonderful sermon. I can safely say everything went very well indeed. Dozens of photos were taken and then we dashed of home for a nosh up. Two very good friends prepared and served the food of which there was plenty. I felt very sorry for them as space was so limited. After we had been fed and 'watered', many of the guests went home to get ready for the reception, later to be held in the Cleveland in Paradise Street, which was managed by friends.
Throughout the day until now I had been in pain. I couldn't take my painkillers because I knew I was bound to have a drink. Well I couldn't not have a drink on my daughter's wedding day. Also, there was this horrid 'undercurrent' in my mind thinking about going back into hospital. I said nothing of this to anyone because I was determined not to spoil Liz's day, and it would have done. It certainly spoiled mine. Alcohol of course, is a powerful painkiller and after a few drinks, I relaxed a bit, but I couldn't stop thinking about my illness. Many friends and relatives were asking me how I was, so it was difficult to forget. Anyway, things

went well into the evening except for a 'low life' who stole Liz's purse while she was dancing with her new husband. We made merry, well into the night, and most of us got sloshed. Everyone, that is, except the bride. The night over, I was informed by my new son-in-law, Chuck, that I had not lost a daughter, I had gained a son and grand-daughter. So now I had two grandaughters - Cheryl-Ann and Lily Mary - named after guess who? I'm sure that was a bribe to secure my baby-sitting service, but I won't...I *did.* Oh well.

Chapter 8

DEJA VU

Here we go again. As I walked into the hospital ward, I experienced a distinct feeling of deja vu. Of course it wasn't deja vu, it had happened before.
Ironically, as I write, I realise that today, 28th April 1991, is the fourth anniversary of my discovery of the blunder. How much water had run under the proverbial bridge since that awful day.
I felt so much more confident this time, I did not need to ask questions. I already know. Last time I thought I was going to die, this time I knew I would not. I also knew what to expect with regards to afterpains.
How much better I felt, how much more secure in my own knowledge.
When I hear doctors say they don't want to tell the patient too much in case it frightens them, I want to bang the doctors head against a wall. Don't they realise? Its what what we don't know that scares us.
I didn't really ask any questions this time, except to enquire of my consultant how the operation had gone.
''Fine'', I was told. This time I knew that she couldn't give me results, that she, like me, must wait for the laboratories to report on their findings. How much easier it was for everyone to know.
After the first operation, they kept me waiting nearly seven weeks for the result. Those were the longest seven weeks of my life. Because of this, I can really and truly

sympathize with women who contact me and who are waiting for results. It is a heart-rending time for, although you know that they can treat most kinds of cervical cancers, you also know there is a slight chance that the results may bring bad news. If only we could persuade them to make more resources available to enable doctors to give results more quickly. If only!
I was told to return in three weeks for my results, not too bad. Anyway, time would fly for me. There was the Internal Review report to be published soon. Also, we were preparing for the legal aid appeal. Three week would soon pass.

The highlight of this hospital stay was a request on the Johnny Kennedy show for me. Little Pat Kirwan had rang Johnny and asked him to play something for me. She sent her best wishes and hoped that I would have a speedy recovery.
I was really touched by this. Liz brought me a little transister radio in, and the other patients and I gathered round my bed. Some of the nurses also listened in. As Johnny spoke Pat's message, I could feel my eyes filling up. What a lovely, thoughtful thing to do. Such were the feelings of closeness felt by all of the recall women for each other.
Many recall ladies were professional people. Most of them, because of their job perhaps, would not take legal advice. I met one such lady while I was in hospital. She was having a cone biopsy. We swapped telephone numbers and she said she would let it go, provided she didn't need any more treatment, but would ring me if she did. I presume she was O.K., because she never did contact me.
The problem for professional ladies was the 'promiscuity tag', because no matter how innocent one might be, mud

sticks.
Even some of the non-professional ladies would not take the matter further, because their husbands would not allow them to. One lady's husband told her: "I'm not having people talking about you!"
With attitudes like that, is it any wonder we are having trouble gettting rid of the promiscuity tag. We must stand up and be counted, we must have faith in ourselves. I do not consider that I have been promiscuous I was never an angel, but definitely not promiscuous. Anyway, what is promiscuity? What does it mean? Is it having sex with a lot of different men? Or is it having a lot of sex with one man? If the latter, then I suppose I must confess to being guilty! Seriously now, a famous well read and well versed doctor from Dublin wrote in his paper on cervical screening, and I quote...........
"It seems that promiscuity, if it means anything is having more sex than the investigator." (Journal, *Clinical Epidemiol.* 1988.)
I wrote a paper myself on the subject, which I entitled, *The Judgement of Hippocrates?*
In it I made several points about cervical cancer and alleged promiscuity. I said that while men are allowed, even encouraged to 'sow their wild oats', women would 'pay for *his* sins.'
If no woman will oblige, then how are men to sow their wild oats? I would ask men to consider this when labelling women 'slags'. Of course, even going back to the early bible days, who got the blame for eating the apple and tempting Adam? A mere woman, and bearing in mind that in those days, women did not count, women were nothing! So, we have big strong Adam being tempted by a mere nothing! I'll leave the rest to your imagination.
Home again, I took things easy for the first week as advised

by the medics. We had our fortnightly women's group meeting of course. I did some studying, but not much more.
Monday, 7th September, business as usual. I again spoke to the Women's Labour Council meeting. Cathy Wilson gave me the name of a man from the unemployed resource centre who was prepared to help me with photocopying the leaflet I had written about the legal aid appeal. Cathy was quite a character. She was very committed to women's issues and was a very strong person in herself.
The man, Jim McCarthy, knew one of the recall women personally. He was quite committed to helped us. He helped us with the leaflets and the posters for our protest outside the place where the legal aid board were to meet. You might be surprised to find that more than a few men were sympathetic to our cause, but not so surprising really when you consider that men are husbands, sons, brothers etc. There were of course, men who thought women were all neurotic, male chauvinist types. Now where have I heard that before?
There was a letter published in our local paper, from Linda Pepper, the member of the Community Health Council who was refused admittance at the Internal review. She made various observations like the fact that she was not connected with any union, she would only have observer status, she would not discuss what she had heard until the report was made public.
She asked: "I also wonder how those 100 women now undergoing urgent treatment feel reading that the purpose of the enquiry is not to establish how the mistake in diagnosis occurred, but rather whether a mistake occurred at all?"
Of course I made straight for my typewriter, and my reply to Linda's inquiry was printed a few days later. I wrote that we, the women were "outraged", and also added: "Mr Fitzpatrick says that the Liverpool Health Authority will not

admit that a mistake has been made, so I wonder, why are the witnesses reluctant to come forward? If no mistake has been made, then what is their problem?''

The days that followed were made up of attending various meetings, and speaking to a variety of people. I was beginning to feel nervous. Time was approaching for the return of my results.

Wednesday, 16th September, we were going to be joined at our usual meeting tonight by some solicitors who had expressed an interest in our proposed campaign efforts regarding the legal aid problem.

I met Max Marcus for the first time. We had seen each other on T.V. We shook hands and I remember saying to him: ''You look much better in the flesh."

He replied: "So do you."

We laughed. He was quite a 'dishy' guy, with nice eyes. I felt he had a warm nature. Have you noticed? I've a 'thing' about eyes. He was in attendance tonight as he represented a number of our members. He walked into the room. His expression was one of faint amusement. Hardly surprising, he was the only man in a room full of women, except for Chris, of course, but Chris was in the kitchen playing 'can-lad'. Again?

Helen also attended, and I met, for the first time, Julie Bradley, Assistant Secretary to the C.H.C.

Julie was accepted instantly by the women, probably because we knew she had an abnormal smear, but no less because she is a lovely person, very warm and sympathetic. She was very ready to share her own experience with us, and to listen to our 'horror stories'.

I felt rather sorry for Max that night, as a solicitor I suppose he had often to listen to intimate details, but surely not in the presence of 19 women. He took it all in his stride.

As I have said, we were making plans to campaign and

demonstrate. Max and Helen guided us, keeping us within the law. I mean it wouldn't have looked too good if we had been arrested. They came to several other meetings. Whenever we needed some kind of general legal advice, they were there.

Here I must also mention Margaret Thompson. What a smashing woman, she gave a lot of help and advice. She helped supply leaflets for our group meetings, and lent me some books etc.

It was probably around this time when I finally accepted that the C.H.C. were really trying to help us, and that they were not 'blagging' us, especially Margaret and Julie. But in all fairness, I didn't have so much contact with Linda and Sylvia. Anyway I saw them more as the 'fighting force', with the former two ladies as the peacemakers, the calming force.

I go on a bit, don't I? But there are so many people I have never had the chance to thank and I want them to know I have not forgotten. Also, these people were very much a part of my story.

Friday, 18th .September, results day! I arrived at the hospital with mixed feelings. I wanted so much to be told I was clear, and yet not daring to hope for this. I still had some back pain, and pain in the pelvic areas. I had not attempted to have sex so I don't know if that would have hurt.

As I sat in the waiting room, I could feel the tension building up and when my name was called, I started.

This time I was seen by a registrar, the young lady who had discharged me. The last day on the ward she came on duty at about nine o'clock. She was buzzing around like a honey-bee, still on the ward when we were having tea. I said to her that she must be tired and she replied that she was dying for a cup of coffee. I had lunch and then Chris

came for me. That poor doctor was still there, and as far as I know, she still had not had her coffee.
As I entered the examination room, she smiled: "Good news this time, Mrs. Hopkins, you are all clear." She looked at me, still smiling, I stared back. Was I expected to burst forth in song? I mean no disrespect to this very hard working doctor, but really! How could a smile and a few words wipe out all that had happened this past seven months? I am sorry, but I just didn't believe her. I vaguely remember asking why I was still having pains. She said something about it not having anything to do with my problem or the treatment. That was what they had all said, so why was I having pain?
I was told to return in six months for a follow-up smear. An appointment made, I went home.
When I arrived home, the press were waiting for me. They knew I was expecting my results, and from somewhere, they had found out I was clear. A reporter asked for a statement, and there was a photographer ready to take my picture. They wanted Chris to pose with me, sort of a happy couple photo.
Everyone expected me to be all smiles, but I just didn't feel like smiling. Instead of feeling relieved, I think I felt drained and stunned. We were asked to pose in the rear garden and "would I hug my husband and smile?" I just couldn't raise a smile, that is, until the photographer almost fell into our rather large hydrangea plant. I smiled, and he snapped.
That photograph was in the papers the next day with the caption: "All clear, the happy couple."
Little did they know we were far from happy, and it was to get worse. Chris, you see, thought that by me getting the 'all clear' things would very quickly go back to normal, but it wasn't as easy as that. By things, I mean our sex life

which was non-existent. I had suffered a terrible mental shock, cancer does that to you, and now he thought that I should jump into bed and go back to being 'his little nymphomaniac' just as before. There was no chance of that. I was not the same person. I had changed. I felt different, I acted different. The old happy-go-lucky, laughing, (sometimes moaning) me had been destroyed. Would I ever be the same again? At that moment I didn't think so, and although most people know me for my sense of humour and optimistic nature, they didn't know me before. I know I am not the same person, especially with Chris. I don't think I will ever be the same again. I felt as though the last years of my youth had been stolen. You may think that at forty-five, I was no spring chicken, but I felt young. Now I feel old. The 'loving wife' was still there, but she was trapped inside me, she couldn't get out. She was trapped by bitterness and fear, and deep, deep resentment. Perhaps she didn't want to come out and be loving, because she had been told that it was loving which caused her problem.

Today, almost four years later, I still feel the same. Afraid to come out and be loved, and yet desperately wanting to be loved. I still feel trapped. I am much more knowledgeable. I know he is not to blame, and yet I am not able to show him my love. What will free me? Will I ever be free?

Chapter 9

KEY FINDINGS

Wednesday, 23rd September. The day dawned at last when the Liverpool Health Authority would present and publish their 'key findings'.
I received a letter a day or two prior to this from Mr. Criddle, Head of Administration. Although dated 14th instant, I feel sure that I did not receive it as early as this because if I had, I would have surely questioned the contents and I have no record of having done so. I probably confirmed receipt by telephone.
The contents of the letter were, as follows:

"Dear Mrs. Hopkins,
The report of the Internal Review is to be presented to the Health Authority on 22nd. September, in private session. The Chairpersons of both Community Health Councils, Mrs. Hilary Clarke and Mrs. Sylvia Hikins, have been invited to attend this meeting
The Chairman has asked me to invite you to come to his office on Wednesday 23rd September at 9.00 a.m., when he will be discussing his report with the CHC's prior to a press conference at 10.00 a.m."

The letter ended by saying that they hoped I would be able to come along, and would I let them know.
I also discovered that the press were given a copy of the report on the 22nd. It seemed that everyone had been given

access except the women, who were directly affected by the damned blunder.
Was this their way of 'keeping us in our place'? I wondered.
I am not ungrateful to Mr. Fitzpatrick for inviting me to attend at least a little before the press conference, because I know it would have been much worse if I had been given a copy of the report at the conference. I would have been unable to answer any of the many questions put to me by the press at all. Nevertheless, one hour was not enough time to read the report let alone understand it.
Only the 'key findings' were printed and the Authority's conclusions/recommendations.
There were no witnesses statements given and very little else. The document was enclosed in a pale blue outer cover and looked very lengthy, but when I took it home and had a good look at the actual contents, I realised that it was made to look more substantial by the inclusion of many DHSS circulars and guidelines.
Incidentally, a reporter showed me his copy of the report on the 22nd, but I only had time to read the first page which gave a summary of the report. This was enough to whet my appetite and when I arrived at Mr Fitzpatrick's office next day, I was in an optimistic frame of mind. The summary led one to believe that there was more to follow. This, of course was far from true. Very little else followed except what I have described above. I was somewhat surprised that they had actually named names, but when you think about it, they really had no choice.
Steve Harrison of the *Liverpool Daily Post* had already disclosed the name of the consultant in charge of the laboratory, and obviously, that person must be responsible for whatever goes on there. It also became clear that they had not really told us anything at all. Instead, they had

wrapped the whole thing up very neatly with the following statement:

They concluded that: "Dr. Kathleen Lodge [the Consultant in charge] was guilty of 'a massive error of professional judgement' for which we can offer no reasonable explanation."

The press asked a lot of questions and to be fair, I had to give them fairly evasive replies. Not because I didn't want to be completely truthful with them, but rather because I had not had time to understand the full implications of such an abridged report.

The press conference took place in one of the Health Authority executive suites. The room was overflowing with bodies, there was hardly space to breathe. At one long table, members of the Authority and certain medical persons were seated. The press and television crews were standing at the back. The CHC members and Helen Barry were sort of squashed together wherever they could find seats. I chose to stand at a corner near to an empty table.

Looking at some old footage of T.V. coverage, it looks like many other T.V. conferences, except that I was there. Even looking back over those old tapes, I can still hardly believe that I was actually there. At one point, I was sort of cornered by the press at that top table, mostly radio reporters. They were not unsympathetic, but questions were fairly flying. I suppose it was easier on me that I was able to answer all at the same time, because it would surely have been too taxing if I had to be interviewed by each individual reporter. These people of the press were great. Although they had a job to do, they made it as easy as possible. Whenever it was practical, they would tell, in advance, what they were going to ask, so that I would have time to think about my answer. Obviously, one does not have to think about the truth, but it is so easy to be mis-quoted, and not so easy to retract a statement once it has been made.

I was truthful enough with the press even though I have previously stated that I was rather evasive. I told them that if I was going to raise any questions about the report with the Authority, I would keep them informed and I have. I was later to raise many questions, but this will be covered in another chapter.

We did not react very well to the report, because, although names were given, it was apparent that nothing was going to happen. No one was being punished. The report also gave the name of a person who we had never heard of, Dr. Percy Jones. He was the the administrative head of department, and us such, had certain responsibilities. It was stated quite clearly that he had been told of the problem by the laboratory staff, but had taken no notice. He felt it was not his responsiblity to challenge the opinion of a senior colleague. He wouldn't want to challenge this particular colleague, because he had recommended her for the job.

The full implications of that fact did not really strike home to us in those early days, but looking back, it smacks of 'old boys network'....'jobs for the boys' ....'doctors sticking together' etc.

Both Dr. Lodge and Dr. Jones were now retired and so that was that. The authority couldn't or wouldn't take any action against them and that made us, the women, more determined to sue. It made us very angry that the guilty parties were getting off 'scot-fee' while we were being made to feel that we were the guilty ones. How dare we sue these poor doctors, how dare we try to take money from the NHS? Most people did not realise that when you sue a doctor, it is that doctors insurance company who pays. That maybe is why doctors don't seem to be very troubled when a patient threatens to sue. I believe it is time, in this country, for the law to be changed. I am not too sure whether 'no faults compensation' is the answer, but we certainly need some new laws to protect the patient. I suppose we felt even more angry in view of the fact that legal aid had been refused to some of us women. We were being forced to prove how much we had suffered. We had to find medical experts to provide us of proof of our suffering. The entire onus was on us, and yet, we were the women who had been neglected by this highly paid consultant's actions.

Oh yes, the authority put the blame on Dr. Lodge, but having said that, they did not admit liability leaving us to prove our case. Yes, it was going to be difficult to find medical experts who would be prepared to give evidence, in open court if necessary, against another doctor. It was not a case of a group of women looking for some easy money. It was more a case of us making the authorities aware that they just couldn't make 911 mistakes and get away it with out so much as a by-your-leave.

The authority had not even said they were sorry, not a single word to any of us women. In my particular case, if someone had taken me aside, in private, and explained what had happened, and that they were sorry and would do their best to put right, I do not think I would have sued. But no, they weren't prepared to do anything. Leave it up to us. What could we do?

They must have known how difficult it would be for us, in every sense of the word. They could have had some consideration for our feelings and distress.

They had accused me of causing panic. They had no idea at all. There was panic among the women of Liverpool, but it was caused by the authority's lack of responsible action. Let's be honest. It is bad enough finding out that you need treatment for cancer, but finding out from a newspaper, or the telly, well that is the limit. I could tell you women queuing up in their place of work, to ring the number given in the press, trying to find out if their names were 'on the list'. I could tell you about women asking family, friends, neighbours to ring on there behalf because they were too scared to ring themselves. I could tell you of women sticking ther 'head in the sand' because they were terrified, of women who were comforting others who had been recalled only to find out at a later date that they, themselves were also 'on the list'.

Oh yes, there was panic, and who could blame us. Other 'errors' were coming to light. They were popping up all over the place.

One case in the news was of a woman who had been having regular smears, and who had died of cervical cancer. But we were told that her tests had not been analysed at the Women's Hospital. They had been sent elsewhere. So it wasn't just the Women's where blunders were taking place, it was at other laboratories too. No wonder we were afraid.

Even women who had been tested outside the 'blunder period', that is 1983-85, were worried in case they had got it wrong with other smears as well. Who can blame the women for feeling that way?

There was a lot in the news about under-funding and under-staffing in laboratories all over the country, but that is clearly not what went wrong in Liverpool. The laboratory staff *got it right*, so it was certainly not a laboratory error as such. Dr. Lodge had a 'formidable' reputation. What did that have to do with it? I know a lot of people who are 'formidable'. Some people think I am formidable but it does not follow that such a person would automatically not make mistakes, although in my experience, formidable people are generally more conscientious. Was she too old? Was she

ill? Many questions would need to be asked, but who was going to supply the answers?
The press had a 'field day', with headlines like:
"Doctor blamed for Test Blunder", "911 massive mistakes", "Clash of opinions opened file on lab errors" "Consultants Blunder - the Mystery Deepens" and many more too numerous to mention. The Internal Review Report hit most newspapers. There was also coverage by all radio and Television stations. I had an interview with *Radio Merseyside* at 11.15 a.m. and one with *Radio Four* immediately after, then there were various T.V. interviews.
I had arranged, with Mr. Fitzpatrick, to pay a visit to the laboratory at the Women's Hospital next morning. Little did I know then that I wouldn't be making that visit until the day after next.
It had been a tiring day, and it wasn't over yet. When I finally arrived home, there was a telephone call from *B.B.C. Breakfast Television.* They wanted me to travel to London to appear on the morning show. I agreed. So they said they would ring me back with arrangements. In the meantime, *T.V. A.M.* rang asking me to appear on their show. I explained that the 'other side' had invited me and they asked that if they could 'sort it out' with the 'other side' would I be prepared to appear on both shows. I agreed that I would. I wanted to get our side across to the people. The press were fine. I have no complaints or criticism at all about them, but statements had to be edited, and quite often that meant they 'cut' the part of your statement out that perhaps you felt was the most important. I understand of course, that editing is essential, as space is limited, but *Breakfast T.V.* was live, just what I needed. I didn't think I would be nervous. I had been on T.V. quite a lot, and I would be quite calm and able to speak clearly, without

nerves getting in the way. As I have described before, nerves make you say things differently to what you want.
As it was quite late by this time, *T.V. A.M.* had arranged to run me to London by taxi. They had booked me into a hotel and said they would send a car to take me to the studio next morning.
I didn't really think about the long journey to London in a car. I didn't have time to think. I had to rush upstairs and pack a few things in a suitcase, sort out the family, have a bite to eat and off.
I needn't have worried about the journey, the taxi driver was fantastic. He took such good care of me even to the point of sharing his coffee and sandwiches. He offered to buy me something in the cafe, but said he didn't like the idea of me going into such a place so late at night. When I wanted to go to the loo, he waited outside, obviously, there some strange people around. He looked after me just like a father. He wasn't old enough to be my father but he was protective enough to have been. I don't suppose it is right for me to mention the name of the firm, some people might think I am advertising, but if I ever had to make a long journey late at night, travelling alone, I would feel quite confident in a Davy Liver Cab.
When we arrived in London, the driver told me to stay in the cab while he checked the hotel. It was just as well, because there had been a change in bookings. He found out where I should go and then took me there. Let's be honest here, he was being paid to drive me to a certain place. He could have dropped me off outside my arranged destination and gone home, but no, he made sure I was O.K. fully booked in and safe. I realise he was being paid for the job, but you can't 'pay' someone for being so nice and caring, you can only say *thank you*, and mean it.

I am not blaming the T.V. people for this slip-up. By the time they had discovered what had happened, it was too late to contact me. I was already on my way, and being such a long journey, we were out of radio contact.
I had been booked in to the Holiday Inn, my room was comfortable, and I was told if I wanted a meal, I only had to ask. I was too tired to eat, but I had a pot of tea sent up. I asked for an alarm call to wake me at 4am. I was being collected at 5.30am. and I wanted to shower and have a cuppa before I left.

Chapter 10

GLASGOW SMILES BETTER

Tring, tring. Not already, it can't be my alarm call. I haven't even been asleep yet.
"Your early morning call, madam" said a pleasantly cultured voice. "Thank you," said sleepy little me. I looked at my watch, it was 4.05 am. I got up straight away. If I had lain back down I would surely have dropped off again.
I asked for some tea and toast to be sent up. While I was waiting, I showered and dressed.
After breakfast, I slapped on some war paint and tried to do something with 'the head'. My hair had always been easy to manage, but lately, it was a real problem, it seemed to 'just hang'. I also seemed to be losing it, coming out by the handful it was. People thought I had Chemotherapy. I suppose it was the worry. Bits of me seemed to have puffed up, and other bits looked drawn and haggard. I must sound like a big-headed bitch. I always had good skin and was good with the make-up, and I liked to make the most of myself, so if that is big-headed, then so be it. What it boils down to is that I didn't like the idea of people feeling sorry for me and I still don't. My outward and humourous nature in public very effectively hid my deep depression and fears. No one will ever realise how I felt deep down when I was alone, but who knows, perhaps writing about it will help. God knows I am finding it difficult enough. How can I make you feel the way I did without being over-dramatic or over the top, and yet I must try, because all of us women

felt the same. We just reacted differently. Some were able to cry or scream, others turned into themselves. Others took it out on their husbands (some of the husbands deserved it for their lack of understanding and demands, but others were very good). I suppose I took it out on my husband by my refusal to even think about sex, but how could I think about sex when I was eating painkillers like smarties at times? I just don't know how it's going to end.

I arrived at the BBC Studios, and was met at reception by a young lady. She led me through a maze of corridors and stairways. I felt fine, until I was shown into the actual studio where they read the morning news. It was like a giant barn. The entire ceiling seemed to be covered in millions of bright lights, and the camera's! Oh no, they were everywhere, at ground level, and at various other levels, right up to the ceiling it seemed. Everywhere I looked, there was a camera. This was my first time in a T.V. studio, and if I felt nervous with the cameras at home, I can't describe how I felt here. As I looked across to the area where I was being led, I noticed the two newsreaders, all dicky-dolled up and looking very suave, sitting in front of a most attractive backdrop.

I was shown to a seat beside the Presenter who was going to interview me. He introduced me to his colleague and both men smiled. They wanted to know my views on the Internal Review and my thoughts on the recommendations of the Health Authority. Unbeknown to me, Mr Fitzpatrick was in the Manchester studio. Had I the courage to look around, I would have seen him on the monitor screen. If I had looked around, I think I would probably have run out. This was a most nerve-racking experience for me. I have never been so nervous in my entire life, not before and not since. I am surprised I was able to speak, although loooking over old video footage, you can tell how nervous I

was. I kept licking my lips and more than once, I stuttered. I am not normally given to stuttering, but I did that day.
I was asked if I was satisfied with the new guidelines and with the new quality control system which was now being practiced at the laboratories. I replied that I was not entirely happy. The Presenter asked what I was unhappy about.
"We don't trust them, that's it in a nutshell." said I. I said we wanted actions, not words on paper. How could they expect us to be confident just because they were telling us that it would be alright from now on? No, we needed more than that.
Mr. Fitzpatrick was brought into the conversation at that point. I thought he looked quite put out by my statement. He said that I was supposed to have visited the laboratory that same morning but realised that I wouldn't be coming. I was being invited the next day, or the one after. I certainly wanted to have a look at the laboratory and talk to the staff. As far as I was concerned, the staff were the stars of the show. Would Dr. Smith have looked at those smears if the staff hadn't brought it to his attention?
I was asked to endorse Mr. Fitzpatrick's new recommendations, and that women should not be put off from going in for smear tests. I had no choice. I had to endorse his views because I didn't want anyone to be put off from having the test just because of what had happened to us. I still saw the smear test as a life-line for women and felt that although there were snags in the system, it was better than no system. We would just have to work hard and campaign for a *safer* system. Until then, women would at least have some protection.
When the Presenter asked me to endorse Mr. Fitzpatrick's remarks, by mistake, he called me 'Mrs. Fitzpatrick'. I couldn't very well correct him on live T.V., but I had a laugh when I got home. I wonder if Mr. Fitzpatrick also

found it amusing?
That interview over, I had to race across London to the *T.V. A.M.* studios. I had left the BBC feeling somewhat 'used'. I didn't really want to endorse any of the Authority views until I had them to study the report, but I couldn't say that I didn't because that would have been the same as saying to the women viewers, "don't go for smear tests", and that might have tragic consequences, so I had to let it go.
I was introduced to Ann Diamond. I found her to be very nice. I believe she was genuinely interested, and appalled at the blunder. I told her how I felt about the 'other side' and asked if I was also going to be asked to do the same here? She asked me what I wanted to say, and I replied: "The truth".
She asked me to tell my story from the beginning, including my feelings about the report. She asked me how I felt having acted responsibly by going for my smear tests as we are all told to do and then discovering that I had been cheated out of the truth.
I replied: "Outraged, furious, terrified."
I went on to say that I could have died. I also said that I didn't want anyone to be put off from having the test but mentioned 'snags in the system', and that I would not be silenced. That part is certainly true. I haven't shut up since, nor do I intend to until we have the whole truth, not the bits they want us to know.
Most of the people I met from T.V. land were very nice. When they are in front of the camera, they are paid to make sure that one is comfortable, and to ask certain questions, but they don't have to do that when they are behind the camera. Many of them did. It made me feel good to think that the faces I see every day on the T.V. are really caring people. They showed a genuine concern for my well-being and for that of the other women.

T.V. A.M. was to continue a twelve-month long cervical cancer campaign, and while I didn't agree with all their guests, I still thought it was a good idea to make women aware of their health needs.
I received quite a few letters following my appearances on T.V., from worried women all over Britain, asking me to visit their home town to try to start off a campaign there. Seven of these were from Glasgow, the city of my birth. Thinking about Glasgow, I should tell you of the panic I caused my poor Auntie Sarah and my cousins. I didn't let them know about my cancer problem. Firstly because there just wasn't time to think in the early days, and later, because I didn't want to put it in writing. I was thinking of paying them a visit when I was well enough. I didn't realise that T.V. programmes were televised nationwide, and the first they knew of my problem, was when they saw me on the telly. I was inundated with telephone calls from worried relatives. How could I have been so thoughtless? It wasn't me being thoughtless, not really, it was more panic and so much happening in such a short space of time. I re-assured them that I was out of danger and promised that I would visit in the very near future. Auntie Sarah was my oldest and closest blood relative since my mum had died and she felt somewhat responsible for me. She had also helped to raise me, she looked after me when my mum was working, so she was like a second mum. She spoilt me rotten when I was little. I owe her a great deal.
I had decided to visit Glasgow as the first stop in a series of visits to other cities. Many of the women who had written, had also telephoned. There was certainly panic all over Britain. I wasn't quite sure what I could do to help all these women, but I think at the back of my mind I had an idea of starting off some kind of groups, for support, and campaigning efforts.

There should have been no need for such actions, but it had become obvious that the authorities were not taking things seriously enough to put our minds at rest.

One of the ladies who contacted me was Lynne from Glasgow. She rang me with a tale so awful, and was very distressed by what she had been through, I told her of my intentions to visit my Aunt. She asked if we could meet. She was looking to the possiblity of starting a help-line or something similar for the women of Glasgow As luck would have it, she lived near to my cousins James and Bettie in Garnethill.

James and Bettie were anxious to help and they did. They arranged several meetings in and around Glasgow so that I could speak to as many people as possible in a relatively short space of time.

They also broadened my horizons by introducing me to ladies from the Chinese, Indian and Pakistani communities. I discovered that language was not the only barrier. There just wasn't enough information around for anyone, regardless of their origin. When I returned home, I would investigate. I wanted to send them leaflets written in their own language. I was surprised to find there were very few. I don't believe the authorities anywhere had taken this aspect into consideration. I also learned there are many difficulties for women from other cultures about having smear tests, mainly I thought because there were not enough female doctors available. I mean most women, regardless of their origin, might prefer a woman doctor to carry out this very personal test, but there was no real choice., most doctors are men. The problem is that some of these women were just not allowed to be examined by a male doctor, for cultural and religious reasons, and so they just didn't go for the test.

James and Bettie worked in their local community centre

and it was part of the job to help the ethnic minority groups, but they also had many friends among these people. I spent many hours of interesting conversations and I learned a lot during this visit to my home town. I was to make a second journey there in 1988. Lynne also comes back into my story then.

My one complaint about that visit to Glasgow was the food. Oh not that there was anything wrong with it. Quite the opposite. But you see, Auntie Sarah was horrified at how much weight I had lost, and had decided to 'fatten me up' while I was there. She fed me extremely well with lots of yummy grub, all the things she knew I liked. For example, empire biscuits, snowballs, and Scottish rolls. Cousins James and Betty had the same idea, and whenever I was with them, they stuffed me with goodies - delicious Chinese meals and lovely broccoli and fish. I honestly don't know where I put it all. I can only say I enjoyed every spoonful, and more than that, I enjoyed being spoiled. Even when I was leaving on the coach, Auntie Sarah gave me loads of lovely ham rolls to eat on the way, and I did.

I've jumped the gun here. I should have told you about the visit to the laboratory. Instead I got carried away. Who wouldn't, with all that Loving Tender Care!

Chapter 11

BRIDGE-BUILDING

My visit to the laboratory was described as a "Bridge-Building exercise" by the *Sunday Times*, under the headlines....
"SCARE OR SCANDAL? "
'Women, living with the fear.'
It was an un-disguised attempt on the part of the Authority to engage my help in restoring public confidence, and one in which I was only too happy to oblige, not only if they could restore my confidence. I was certainly not going to lead the public up the garden path. I was not prepared to tell people that things were great if I did not feel that way myself. There had been enough secrecy and hiding of the facts. I would not tell the public anything I did not feel and believe.
Although I went to the laboratory with an open mind, I was also rather sceptical about what I would see and hear.
By now, I was accustomed to hearing their long words and having statistics thrown around to prove this and that, but that was not what I was looking for. That would not satisfy me. I wanted plain and straightforward facts, laid squarely on the table, and that is not exactly what I got, but let me tell you-what it was like.
I was introduced to Dr. Peter Smith and his staff by Mr. Pearse Butler, the new manager. Mr. Butler was quite a young and likeable sort of chap. He did not have the finesse, or command as such people as say, Mr. Fitzpatrick, the Chairman, but that was quite understandable. He was

probably fairly new to the job, and had taken over at a very awkward time. He must have felt rather like a Christian being thrown to the lions.

The immediate general atmosphere was very tense. I shook hands with Dr. Smith, who smiled and said "How do you do?" I was led by the two men throught the actual laboratory.

Helen Barry accompanied me on that visit. She too was very interested in what we would find, but probably for different reasons.

Dr. Smith is very good-looking, and very tall. He must stand at 6'4", give or take an inch. He seemed quite pleasant but was obviously nervous, not that I could blame him. He 'talked' us round the laboratory, stopping to explain certain things here and there. Mr. Butler made various references to the new openness enjoyed by Dr. Smith with his staff. Certain members of staff confirmed this. Really speaking, what else could they do? I mean they couldn't very well say in front of the superiors, that they didn't agree. I was introduced to two senior Medical Laboratory Scientific Officers, to give them their correct title (MLSO'S) who also made some comments.

When there a gap in the conversation, Mr. Butler would fill in with his 'bridge building'.

I would not hold that against him. After all, that was his job, and one he was doing very well, and no, I am not being patronising.

I didn't really have a free reign to speak to whoever I wanted. It was pretty much a pre-arranged affair, only to be expected don't you think? Nevertheless, I did manage to pick up on quite a lot.

Body language is a very useful means of communication, and never more so than on this occasion. Pearse Butler acted like a cat on a hot tin roof, Peter Smith like a wimp.

Wringing his hands and licking his lips would have seemed more appropriate on a small weedy character, and he was certainly not that. He is not wimpish in any sense of the word. He is a fine figure of a man. And there is nothing wimpish about his character either. He stood up to the might of the medical profession, his own colleagues, and that would be no way easy. It was probably more difficult for him than for me, being an outsider and not having to work with them. Although he took his time, he did it. He brought the whole thing into the open, no mean task in his position.

I make no apologies for my description of the two men. I do it so that the reader may have an idea of the atmosphere that day. Everyone was very nervous and the air was frought with tension. They rather reminded me of actors who were afraid that they might forget their lines. Am I being unfair? Was I being influenced by my own scepticism? I really don't know, but I have to say how I felt.

Helen Barry felt some of the tension too, but was not quite as suspicious as me about every word and every gesture. It was a new experience for me being surrounded by professionals. Helen on the other hand is a professional herself and so may be more used to them. I should imagine that the atmosphere would be similar in the court-room during a trial, when waiting for the jury to return. She did however agree that the episode was somewhat 'stage-managed'. I doubt if it would have been any different if had just walked in off the street. It might have been worse.

The laboratory staff were the 'shining stars' of this fiasco as far as I am concerned. They were the first to discover that something was wrong from the start, as early as three months after Dr. Lodge took up her appointment. Of course, as we all know, no one would listen to them. I shudder to think what would have happened if Dr. Lodge's appointment had been a longer one! I doubt if I would be writing this book, and approximately twenty-four other women might have been helping me to push up the daisies, maybe even more. Who knows, or will admit?

It must have been a nerve-racking experience for those who I met that day which I feel is very unfair. They were being put on the rack, while the real 'baddies' enjoyed retirement. It's a funny old world, isn't it!

Despite those sweating palms, wrung-out hands and lip-licking exercises, I did pick up on one good vibration. Dr. Smith and his staff were displaying more openness. They even laughed with each other, something which I doubt would have happened in the laboratory when Dr. Lodge was in charge. They were proud of their new equipment, a five-headed microscope. I was allowed to have a look myself, not that I fully understood what I was looking for, not in those early days. I would now, but then I have had three more years of study. Perhaps I should request another visit. Maybe I will.

The *Sunday Times* concluded by saying that I was "happy to endorse smear tests, believing that any check system is better than no system at all," and that we were committed to campaigning for a better ssystem.

They also mentioned the unique 'New Zealand Experience', a medical study which lasted for twenty-eight years. Whereby a 'God-like' creature in a white coat decided that pre-cancer had nothing to do with invasive cancer, the kind which kills. As a result, hundreds of women either had no treatment, or inadequate treatment resulting more than a few deaths and many more women had to have extensive treatment. I do not have space to discuss this more fully here, but suffice to say I was totally disgusted with the entire affair, not only because of the way the women were treated, but also because most of the medical world knew of and disagreed with the 'white coated god'. Having said that, they all sat back and did nothing. A striking example of lack of medical ethics and doctors 'sticking' together, if ever there was one. Just what are these people about? Are they there to save lives or their colleagues' face? One must ask, and one must wonder! Why do they bother to take the Hippocratic Oath if they are not going to abide by it? It would seem to be a case where they pick and choose which rules to observe. For example, they observe the rule which says they should not impart their knowledge to anyone who is outside the profession excepting their own sons, but they sometimes ignore the rule which says they must treat patients to the best of their ability and knowledge. Surely that means that they should not withold treatment for a patient in order to prove their own, or other people's theories. That is what happened in New Zealand.

Our local headlines ....

"MY HEROES, by woman caught up in smear test fiasco." and "Cervical Cancer Victim says 'THANK YOU' - both quite appropriate, I thought, because I did thank them, and they *were* 'my heroes'.

Another local headline....

"Health Chief's bid to quell cancer smear test fears", quoting a well-known gynaecologist as saying: "We do believe that in Liverpool, we have a service as good as anywhere else," was probably quite true, but really, it had nothing to do with what happened at the Women's Hospital, in my opinion, as you will see when you read my last chapter.

My visit ended, I walked out of the laboratory with Helen and Pearse Butler. Helen walked on ahead while Mr. Butler and I stopped to have a conversation at the top of the outside steps, more for the benefit of the television cameras than anything else, I thought.

I was interviewed by certain television companies and by *Radio City*. I gave the same interview basically to all. I said that I "wouldn't be satisfied with just one visit", and that when I was fully satisfied, I would be happy to report to the public. I ended by promising to 'stick on in there' until I had found out the truth.

I am still 'in there' but sadly I am no nearer to revealing the truth now after three years. than I was on that day. I am not going to stop fighting for the truth, no way. It is just taking longer than I thought, bearing in mind that time, in the medical world, is not exactly the same as time to us mere mortals.

The last two days of September were taken up with helping and supporting Mrs. E.. who visited at home, and with our group meeting.

It was only three weeks until the legal aid appeal, and tension was mounting once again. It didn't matter whether or not we were personally affected by the appeal, as I have said before, we worried for each other. I often laughed when I thought of the situation we were in, especially when you think about the doctors. We are always being told that stress and trauma are 'contributary factors' in cervical cancer, and yet, look what they were putting us through.

When some of us asked how we got the disease, we were told, "you must have been playing around" or a similar term of phrase.

The authority were admitting that it was a "massive error of professional judgement" but saying 'we are not liable'. So we turned to the law, and now they were telling us "you have not suffered enough to quantify damages". How could we avoid being stressed? How were we supposed to feel? Perhaps we should take it 'lying down' (excuse the pun) or forget the whole thing. Maybe they thought that is

what we would do, but no chance! They were just not on. We would fight through to the bitter end for the truth and justice. That is all we want. We don't want any favours, although maybe they owe us some for what they have put us through. It doesn't matter who's fault it was, it was clearly not ours. We had acted in a responsible fashion as recommended by the department of Health, but where had it got us? I feel very angry every time I hear them saying "Two thousand women die each year from cervical cancer, most of them have never had a smear." What a joke! Here in Liverpool were nearly one thousand women who had come in for a smear, and look at us now! How could they justify their words? Granted, most of us hadn't died, but that was surely a case of 'there but for fortune'.
For the first week in October, my diary was bulging. I sometimes had for or five different appointments or things to do. I don't know where I got the time to write letters, but I did. It is amazing what you can do when you try.

Oct. 1st, Pop in to Helens office....Enquire at education re grant for Julie....See Steve.

On the *2nd*, I paid a home visit to a lady who needed advice but was too ill to come out.

Saturday 3rd, I visited a new group member in hospital where she was about to have a hysterectomy.

Oct. 5th, Call on Dr. Katie Gardener, (a Liverpool G.P. who was lending me a video to be shown at my group meeting)....Drop in on Anne (group member), Contact Max Marcus, ring two other solicitors, 4.00 p.m. appointment with W, ring council re sink.

The last entry makes me giggle, it looks so out of place, doesn't it?

Oct. 6th.....Ring Jim McCarthy re stall. Jim worked at the unemployed resource centre and was helping us set up an information stall in Church Street to give out leaflets etc.

Oct. 7th, I attended a Liverpool Health Authority meeing in the company of the CHC. I had been going to these meetings once a month because I wanted to learn how the authority worked.
In the evening, I spoke to the meeting of the Aigburth Labour Party, who were kind enough to make a collection for the fund we had launched to help the legal aid women who had to pay a contribution.
Then I had three days 'off'. Great! Now I can catch up on my typing.

14th. Oct, Group meeting, the last we would have before the legal aid appeal. We had to finalise our plans regarding collection and distribution of the leaflets we had prepared, also about our 'peaceful' demonstration. Again, some people didn't want to come, because they knew there would be media coverage. Some were not well enough to walk or stand around, but even so, we had ample coverage planned. Max and Helen were present, again to ensure that we stayed on the 'right side of the law'. Not that we planned anything illegal, but it is all too easy to fall foul of the law through ignorance. They were marvellous, all the way through those early frightening days, they were there to guide us. Other solicitors were nice enough but they didn't get personally involved the way Helen and Max did. There were also some who didn't think that we should be causing such a rumpus, that we should leave it up to them. We didn't agree with that at all. There had been enough cover up, everyone should know what was going on.

The legal aid appeal was to be heard at 2 p.m. on October 21st at the head office of the Law Society in James Street. We had arranged to meet ouside at 1 o'clock. I had to call into Helen's office and collect the leaflets from the unemployed centre, who were kindly photocopying them for us before I joined the others. I met 'Paula' at Helen's office. She was one of the ladies whose case was to be heard. There had been something in the newspapers that morning and some coverage by the local radio. We didn't get the full coverage we might have, because there had been a national disaster that morning. We nevertheless made ourselves heard. Two or three of us paraded up and down Chruch Street and Lord Street giving out leaflets, also to people going in and out of the Law Society offices. I was jumping on and off buses, giving them to passengers. Yes, I did pay my fare, I had a zone ticket. I don't know what I must have looked like. Something out of the comics. I really didn't think what it was like for the general public, and I mean no offence by that. We just had to find a way of letting the public know of the injustice we felt we were receiving.

Men as well as women come to lend their support that day. Some were relatives of the women, and some were public sympathisers.

Some time after the women involved had been called in, a message was sent out for me to come in. Helen, Max and a couple of the other solicitors met me at the elevator doors. They were smiling broadly.

"We have just received word, the appeal has been granted. We have won." How can I describe my feelings? I hadn't been refused legal aid because my case was more serious, but to see me there, that day, you would have thought I had. I ran into the room where the other women were waiting. There was a lot of kissing and tears and hugging. Smiles all round was the order of the day. The solicitors looked with amused expressions on their faces. Mind you, it must have been quite a sight.

Helen and Max took their clients and me, of course, off to the cafe to 'celebrate' with tea, coffee and buns. Max paid. He insisted.

There were those who wanted me to say that it was our campaign efforts that made the Law Society change their mind, and although I like to think that perhaps we did help in some small way, I prefer to think that what really happened was that the Law Society, at first, decided the women should be given the chance to provide the evidence required to prove their case. Again, it doesn't matter why. The important thing is we were now going to have a chance. Justice had prevailed, at least for now.

Chapter 12

BUSY, BUSY

After the legal aid appeal, I had four days off, apart from a private meeting with one lady. I caught up with my typing, (again?) and my studies. I was becoming quite the little expert. What had Ann Diamond called me? "Bit of an arm-chair expert". Oof, what a title.
Monday, 26th October. Jamie's birthday. He is ten today. How time flies. I joked with him that morning saying that he was getting to be a big boy and that "my son and heir would soon have no hair." he replied. "Go way, mum, I'm not going to be baldy like me dad." At that time, Chris had a bald spot as big as a pin-head, but the kids used to tease him about it. He didn't much like this, and I suppose that is something we women will never understand, the relationship between a man and his hair. They just don't like to lose their hair, and I don't know why. I mean, 'bald men are more sexy', and 'more virile'. Wouldn't you think that they would want to go bald with an image like that?
Now that I have had a 'rest, I'm 'raring' to go, which is just as well because my diary is fully booked up for the remainder of the year, and how.
Judy Graham from *T.V. A.M.* rang to ask me to appear on the show again for sort of an 'update', and I spoke, for the first time, to a group of young people.
I was a bit wary when I discovered that the ages were from 14 to about 19 years. You imagine a lot of giggling and carry on when you speak about the human body and sex to that age group, but no! This group of Young Socialists

from Broadgreen were very responsible. They were most interested in the 'blunder' and asked some very intelligent and pertinent questions. For example, they wanted to know how I had coped, how the other women had coped, at what age should a woman have her first smear, about snags in the system. Now this was a group of boys and girls, and the boys were seriously interested. One young man said: "When I marry, I would like to learn how I can help my wife if she has a problem." He was about 14 years old. We did have a laugh at some points. For some reason or other, people can't help laughing when I am around. (I'll have to stop going out without my make-up!). The young people thanked me and said they had learned a lot. It was a most satisfying meeting for me. I left feeling good. I must say that since then, I have attended many similar meetings of the young, and apart from the odd giggle when you mention certain parts of the body, they have been great. The message that comes across to me is, that our young people want to know. Talking about cancer does not frighten them, quite the contrary. It was hidden from us when were young and we grew up ignorant. Let us not do that to our children.

That Wednesday, I had a meeting with Mr. Fitzpatrick. These meetings were mainly informal. We discussed cervical screening and treatment in a general sort of way.

We couldn't for obvious reasons, discuss individual legal cases, but we were able to talk about the medical side of things to a certain extent. We had an unspoken agreement, that I would tell him what I wanted to discuss on behalf of a particular lady, and he would then say whether he was able to do so, which seemed fair enough to me. Some people might feel that he should have been able to be more open, but we should realise that, as chair, his first duty was to protect the interests of the authority, in much the same way as I felt as a leader of the women. Their interests came first with me.

I found Mr. Fitzpatrick a very interesting and pleasant man to talk to. I know it was difficult for him sometimes. I suppose he often felt like 'piggie in the middle'. I concluded, from our many meetings, that he felt a personal interest and sympathy for our plight, but he had a job to do, and like many people in power, he could not allow personal feelings to influence him.

Our meetings were not always made up of questions, answers, arguments, so I was able to occasionally, see the 'man inside'. Once, when we were having a coffee break, he asked me if I had always had an interest in medicine? I told him that in my youth, I had wanted to be a nurse and that I had been 'put off' by tales of how I would have to deal with dead bodies, and how I had heard that they 'sit up', 'talk' and had been known to 'grab you.' Mr. Criddle, (Administration) who was present told us that he had been a mortician, and confirmed that sometimes bodies do behave in this manner, but that it was unlikely, as a young student nurse, that I would have been left on my own to manage with a dead body. As I'm sure you can imagine, at seventeen, or eighteen, that was my one great fear, so much so that it stopped me from becoming a nurse and I have regretted that decision ever since. On the other hand, if I had become a nurse, I would have been 'one of them' and so might not have been able to do the job I am doing now. God works in mysterious ways, eh? Not that I'm knocking nurses, most definitely not. I, together with millions of others, feel that our nurses are wonderful. In fact, they are my favourite health professionals, and problably the most hardworking too. We all love our nurses, even although you occasionally get a nasty one, or a rough one. Even the sister in Oxford Street Maternity hospital who told me off for hanging my knickers on the radiaor to dry during doctors rounds. Remember me, Sister S.?

There is much excitement in our group this week. We have been asked to take part in a documentary on Channel Four. Many of you may have seen the programme. It was called *Woman in View.* They wanted to come along to interview me first, and then some of the women in the group.

There was 'Susan', 'Sherry', little Pat, and me. We pushed two couches into 'corner' shapes and we sat two on each. Part of the time, we were left to talk amongst ourselves, but sometimes we were asked specific questions. The interview went on for quite a long time so that there would be enough material to edit into a nice neat little package. We were given ten to fifteen minutes viewing, and it's amazing what you can cram into that. We felt that the end result was good. It covered the problems well.

Busy, busy Steve is writing an article about my campaign for the *Bella* magazine. The photographer is due at 2.30 p.m. As you can see, I have stopped being quite so shy about publicity. I have sort of accepted it as 'norm', and it was doing me a power of good. I was invited regularly to speak to women's groups, and that meant a chance to pass my message to even more women: "You must have a smear test!"

Anyway, family, friends, and most other people were used to seeing my face in peculiar places. We used to laugh about it at home. The kids would sing "she's a star, superstar". Then there would be the giggles because I haven't got two pennies to rub together. The women in the group used to tease me as well, but it was 'nice teasing' not nasty.

Now its off to London again. *TVAM* calling. No nice taxi driver this time, just the plain old fashioned train. Different hotel, but just as nice, and this time, I arrived at a respectable hour, not in the middle of the night. I was told at reception, that I could have a meal in the dining room or I could have something sent up to my room. I preferred the latter, as I wanted to go over some papers. I was becoming the 'old hand' at this, television, I mean. I had learned that time is short and you must make the most of that which you are allowed. At least, this time, I knew what they wanted to discuss and I could have some answers ready. It's funny, looking back before the cancer issue, I used to grumble because I couldn't afford to go out for a drink. Not that drink or the lack of it bothers me, but I liked to socialize, and now twice in the same year, I am in a situation where I only have to ask and I shall receive. (I had been told I could have some drinks if I wished) I didn't ask, I wanted to keep a clear head and anyway, I've 'gone off' alcohol in the same way I have 'gone off' many other things since my operations. Ask my husband, he seems to be reminding me a lot these days of what I have gone off, and he doesn't mean drinks either! Oh dear, bitterness creeping in? I'd better change the subject, and I'm doing that quite often at home, as well. Woops!

Back in Liverpool, Thursday 12th November. Our group set up an information stall in Church Street. We had applied for permission to the City Solicitor and this was readily given. What we wanted was to bring leaflets and information onto the street, where women were shopping, so that they would be able to pick up what they wanted instead of having to go to the clinic and ask. There was 'Susan', Donna, 'Annie' and myself. That is one day we won't forget in a hurry. It was blowing gales. We no sooner put the leaflets in place, than they had blown away. It was raining off and on, and if I remember correctly, there was a bit of snow or sleet as well. It was a weird sort of a day really. As well as the weather described above, we also had the sun popping in and out of the clouds. It was *freezing*. Most of the shoppers seemed quite surprised to see us there and were wary of coming over. Not to be wondered at when you think about it. Here we were right in the middle of shops and stalls, all selling their goods and we were giving away free leaflets and information. Nevertheless, I believe it was moderately successful. It would have been better if we had the newspaper coverage we should have had, except that, guess what? There was another national disaster. It was becoming quite a thing. This was the third time, I think, when what we had planned co-incided with such a disaster. Whenever I rang *Radio Merseyside* or *City* to ask them to mention our planned event, they would put extra staff on to cope with whatever may accompany it. It happened five or six times in all. For example the Hungerford Shooting, and the Lockerbie Aircrash. Quite weird. I even tried changing our dates several times. It didn't work. Something would still happen on the same date. One reporter from *Radio City* said to me: "Would you please not plan anything for a few weeks, I haven't had a day off for ages." It got so that I was afraid to make dates, because it was as though I was forecasting the date of a disaster.

First week in December, my visit to Glasgow which I have mentioned earlier, although I don't think I told you about fitting in 15 meetings in four days. How the heck did I do that? I had asked Betty and James to arrange as many meetings as they could. I had to see as many people as I could, and ooh, didn't they do well? I must give credit where due. They worked tremendously hard in the preceding weeks to make the arrangements. Fifteen meetings throughout the city is no mean task. At the end of that week, I knew what 'stars' and 'royalty' meant when they speak of gruelling tours etc., Mind you, I'm not too sympathetic towards them. They travel in comfort. Not like me, 'slumming it' on trains, subways, and buses. I'm only joking, it was tiring but I loved every minute. I found it strangely enlightening to see how things were in another city, and it wasn't only Liverpool that things went wrong! The system was a shambles nationwide. No wonder women from so many cities were writing to me. They wanted the situation high-lighted, they wanted improvements. I made many notes of what I had seen. Hopefully, I could put it all together and make some use of it to help women in general. If not, at least I would make sure that people were aware of the many snags in the system, no matter where they lived.

I have been strangely quiet about the CHC of late. No, not really, I have tried to bring people into the story as they played a part. Margaret Thompson, you remember, the Secretary of the CHC, asked me to write an article for inclusion in their Annual General Report. I said I would be delighted as this report went out to all sorts of people, including the Health Authority. This was perhaps my chance to say things I had not been able to say before, to let them know how I really felt and also what I was doing, plus a variety of other things. My mind runs riot with thoughts. By now, as you may have gathered, I respected Margaret perhaps more than the others at the CHC but then I had more dealings with her than anyone else. Julie Bradley was a 'close second', with Sylvia Hikins coming third. Kind, aren't I. The three women know me well enough now to laugh at what I am saying here. In the early days, I'm not sure what their reactions might have been. Margaret also asked me to be guest speaker at the Annual General Meeting. She called my offering 'My year'. It was a most appropriate title and so I stuck to it.

This was probably my first attempt at writing, and although I was doing it myself, space was still limited. I had been given a certain amount of word space and I simply had to get some feelings in there. I had funny feelings as I wrote that article. It was then when I realised that although I still feel angry about what had happened, that anger would not 'win the war'. I had to change. Maybe I should become 'cold and calculating'? and I was of a mind to be so, but then I would be as they were. Did that mean I was succeeding in what I had set out to do? I had said before I needed to 'think like them', 'know what they knew', etc. In that respect, I had succeeded. I was beginning to be like them, but I also wanted to be sure to keep my feet on the ground, be constantly aware of my basement beginnings, my grass roots. That was absolutely essential, because it was at grass roots level the help was needed, not 'up there with them!'. When I look back, it's incredible the kind of thoughts that went flying through my head, the various feelings I had, such mixed feelings. I suppose it was a necessary part of my 'transition', being able to communicate with 'them up there' and 'us down here'. The one thing I never wanted to forget, was the pain and the anguish of the women, as if I ever could. I was one of them. For me the pain remains to this day. It is etched in my mind as a sort of monument to the poor, dear ladies who I met and got to know during these past four years and who have sadly passed away. The thing that I remember most about them is the lovely gleam of hope in their eyes as they woke to enjoy, mid their pain, another day on this earth. That gleam of hope which shone briefly, in their eyes, is the hope for tomorrow for all women. Together We Stand.

There was television coverage of that meeting, and it had been mentioned that I would like to go into schools to speak to the older girls about the importance of having regular smear tests. In theory, the education department were in favour but it was up to the individual head to make the final decision. Johnny Kennedy mentioned this on his show and said that I would welcome offers. As a result, I was invited to speak to quite a number of young people, but not in schools, in colleges and similar establishments. That was O.K. as I was concerned, I was still getting message to the young, the place was not important. Some school teachers felt that it wasn't necessary to tell school girls as they wouldn't need this kind of instruction yet, but I believed we could not afford to view the situation 'ostrich-fashion'. We had to be realistic. Besides, even if the girls didn't need to actually have a smear test there and then, the seed would be sewn in their young minds, so that when there was the need, they would not be afraid. I was thinking about some of the things we had talked about in the group meetings, how some of us were totally ignorant about the test, and how others hated the thought of having them. I hated the idea of girls growing up to feel frightened and ignorant like we had, and don't forget, I had four daughters. The other women felt the same. I had nightmares thinking about my girls going through what I had gone through. In a typically 'mother-type' way I did not think they would be able to cope. The more rational side of my nature said: "Of course they could cope. You did, and so would they" and more honestly I suppose I didn't want to be placed in the position where I would have to watch them cope.

The newspaper style Annual Report carried a picture of the Women's Hospital on the front page and was headed 'CERVICAL SCREENING BLUNDER', and 'My Year' by Lily Hopkins, with a photograph taken by Margaret at our last group meeting in my front room. We laughed when I refused to pretty myself up for this, but I wanted people to see me as I was. I was wearing a plain short sleeved jumber under a 'tatty' old cardigan. My hair didn't look so good either, but that was me! Margaret understood what I was doing and I think she agreed. I was in my own home, with a group of women who had become my friends. I didn't need to stand on ceremony. The article had quite an impact. I was very glad. I had been a bit nervous writing for such an impressive document as the CHC report. I didn't really want praise but it is useful if you are praised. It tells you you've done a good job and it's hardly worth doing otherwise, is it?

Our last group meeting of the year took place on December 16th. We didn't talk very much about our problems but we had a dirnk and a buttie instead. We resolved to make some very definite plans for 1988 and would meet in January.

New Years Eve was the 'big' thing for me, being Scottish-born I suppose. I didn't go out but stayed home with the kids to 'get the party ready'. Normally, I wouldn't have very much to drink in the early stages. As hostess I would make sure that everything was going well and everyone was having a good time. Then at around 2.30 a.m. it was my time. That meant time for me to get sloshed and dance into the small hours with a chair or an ashtray. (Is that where 'fag-ash' Lil came from?) Later, I would sit on the floor and play all the old sentimental records and cry my eyes out. With fond memories or regret? I don't really know, but that was me. This year I felt rather more subdued. I didn't want to drink. I 'supervised' things but hadn't the heart to join in. I made a go of it for the sake of the family, but I wasn't my usual self. Maybe it was my married life which was getting to me, things had not gone back to normal between Chris and I. I had been given the 'all clear' by the doctors but someone had forgotten to contact my mind. The thought of married love was very far away, I don't know why. I didn't sit down one day and say to myself: "You do not want to make love with your husband". It wasn't like that at all. I can't understand it but my body craved for love and for things to be the way they were, but my mind would not allow this. I would lie awake at night thinking about sex, but as soon Chris touched me I froze. I longed for him to kiss and cuddle me the way he used to, and yet I would push him away when he tried. Maybe if he had just held me in his arms without trying for sex? But he was human too. He had been without for quite some time now, and he had needs, more obvious than mine. Maybe next year?

Chapter 13

SIX CITIES AND ME

My working new year started on 8th January with an interview on *Radio Merseyside* about my trip to Oxford the next day. I was going to meet with a group of women who were also dissatisfied with the system and had started a pressure group. Their particular concern was the waiting time for colposcope. That is the next stage in medical assessment after you have had an abnormal smear, and naturally would want this to follow as quickly as possible in case you have a serious problem. In their area, the waiting time was about nine months, and their worry was they might be walking around with cancer for that time. Then of course, they worried because they may also have had to wait for treatment.

Jan Gauntlett - you remember, the Laboratory manager - came back into my life during that trip. She met Helen and I in London and drove us through to Oxford to meet the ladies.

We had a most interesting and informative day, exchanging notes and views. We were all working towards the same goal, a better system for all women. I said I was trying to do something on a national level and we agreed to keep in touch.

The next stop was Manchester. I had a number of calls and letters from the area and this visit was to see what was available to women there. I visited places like the Community Health Council, and CALL, a support group for cancer sufferers. I looked around at posters and clinics with the idea of compiling information to be passed on as required. There was a young woman in the Greater Manchester area who was interested in starting off a group to cover abnormal smear cases.

Then, another week in Glasgow. You see, I went where the interest was greatest or where the need seemed to be, but obviously, I needed a personal contact, someone to arrange meetings etc., in their own area. I would have found it pretty impossible to do that from Liverpool. Even if I'd had the money to work with and I did not. Fortunately, there was no shortage of willing hands. Everywhere I went, women were crying out for help, support or just information.

I decided to arrange a meeting in Liverpool to get us all together. I called it a "National Group Meeting". It was held at the offices of the Community Health Council in Whitechapel. As you may have gathered, I now accepted that the council really were there to help the patient. They were not merely 'lackies' put there by the authority to fob people off and I'm afraid that is what I thought in the first place.. They in fact do a great job, and are still doing it. I believe this sincerely, so much so that I have recently become a member of that self same council myself, and no, it is not highly paid. We get no wages, but it is a very satisfying and worth-while position.

The National Meeting was attended by ladies from four other cities. We compared notes and discussed our best way forward. Actually, just by meeting, we were saying to health authorities everywhere: "We are not prepared to take what you are giving us. We want a better system and are able and willing to fight for it if necessary. We were able to attract some publicity which certainly helped. The more publicity, the more those in authority would realise that we were quite serious. This was not just a 'flash-in-the-pan' idea.

Durham was my next port of call, and was I pleasantly surprised with that city. A lady from that area had written to me after one of my *TVAM* appearances. She said there was some interest in her area. The system was a 'bit iffy'. After corresponding for some months, I asked whether it would be useful for me to come through. She replied that it certainly would, and offered to put me up and arrange some meetings for me. She did all of this and wouldn't take a penny for my food. I would love to tell you her name. Sadly, I have lost touch with her in recent months and can't therefore ask her permission. I doubt she would mind if I just tell you that her christian name is Sylvia.

Through Sylvia, I was able to meet the Durham Womens Pressure Group who were there basically to promote and support womens issues. Also, someone from the Lesbian Mothers group, and a lady who lived near Durham who wanted to start a self-help group.

I seem to have 'wandered' again. I was telling you I was surprised when I arrived in the city. I am not too sure what I expected, but thinking of the song 'Durham Town' one thinks of Durham as an industrial town. I can tell you it doesn't look that way at all. It is a most beautiful city, with a wonderful Cathedral, and delightful people. I spent only two days there and I would just love to go again. While I was waiting for my train, I had a couple of hours to spare. Sylvia accompanied me into the city centre and then she had to go to work, so I went into the Cathedral. I could happily have stayed there for hours. The architecture and just the 'feel' of the place were great. There was a little bridge and a river overlooked by the university, deep and winding streets leading down to a wondrous city centre shopping area. So clean and fresh looking. Not the way one would imagine a industrial city at all. I mentioned my thoughts to Sylvia. She said most people say the same. And so unlike the words of the song, I didn't want to leave old Durham town.

In March, came my first visit to speak of, to London town. My, what a place. I love London, but I don't think I would like to live there. Too fast. I was speaking at a meeting of the TUC in Lambeth. Once again, I came across Jan. We made plans to meet at a later date because apparently, she had 'certain plans'.

Later that month, I spoke to the Annual General Meeting of the Liverpool Labour Womens Council. There were numerous radio broadcasts, and newspaper interviews throughout the year. They followed me wherever I went. This made me feel elated, but very humble at the same time. O.K., they were doing a job, making a living, but there were plenty of more 'exciting' stories going around. No matter what was in the news at any given time, they still found space for news of the Liverpool cancer smear blunder. I think this shows the extent of concern among people in general for what had happened to us women. Even today, four years on, the press still keep in touch, and help where they can. It's more than their job to many of them, they really do care.

We had started to hold house parties selling make-up, clothing and in fact anything that was legal and moral. Oh dear! I'm forgeting, the naughty nighties parties, are they moral? We are not sure and don't care because although these parties didn't bring in a lot of cash, they certainly lifted our morale!!

I continued to attend and speak at meetings including one at City College, to a group of women 'taking a second chance' at learning. I visited breast screening units, various different support groups. Wherever there were people, you would find me. It is amazing what you can learn just by being present.

I even attended a meeting of the Home Watch, should have been the Body Watch.
A new slant was creeping into the invitation scene. I was getting calls from G.P.s and other health professionals who had become interested in my work. They were beginning to see that women sometimes needed more than professional help, and that a shoulder to cry on was not such a bad idea after all. They also saw that I wasn't just running around 'scandal-mongering' or reading the riot act. I genuinely wanted to help women to come to terms with, or understand better what was happening to their bodies. Some were even happy to give my phone number to their patients. This is exactly what I wanted. If it was difficult to work with them, it was just as difficult to work without them, no useful purpose was being served by a 'them and us' situation.
Another week long visit to Glasgow taking in ten meetings, some of them with professionals, and then rush home for our own group jumble sale. A fun day at Sefton Park, fundraising, of course, squeezing family activities in between. And so the year progressed.
Off to Birmingham now, to meet with some health professionals, and to visit a lady with whom I had been corresponding, and who tragically, was dying. She had three little children. What a woman! So brave and yet so sad. The courage I have seen over these past four years. Is it any wonder I am filled with incentives. How could I stop campaigning now with all these sad/happy memories, sometimes heart-wrenching and horrifying like the one which still stands out in my mind, of the little boy of seven who's mummy had just passed away, and who ran screaming from the room: "I hate Jesus, he took my mummy away." His dad had told him that "mummy was with Jesus, now" to try to soften the blow. How can you

soften the blow for a seven year old child when he has just lost his mum? The answer is, you can't! This sort of case to me, is like fuel to a fire-fly. It makes me so angry because I know that his mummy should not have died. She had regular smears. It makes me all the more determined to make them see what they are doing to us with this joke of a system.

Then there was the Manchester Blunder which never happened. Let me explain if that is possible. It came out eventually that it was not a blunder, it was something to do with 'quality control', at least, that is what we were told. I was in Manchester quite a lot these days. Mostly visiting women in their own homes, or 'snooping around'. There were things being leaked to the press about laboratories and smear test 'mix-ups'. It was difficult to know what was true, and what was for some 'inside' benefit. Nevertheless, I was there, just in case. I wasn't prepared to leave anything to chance.

A visit to Blackburn in August, and then later in the month I'm off to London again to take part in a sponsored walk for a cancer charity. I can't go into details again because I haven't got the person's permission, but it was quite well publicised at the time. It took place in London Hyde Park and my photograph appeared in the *Liverpool Daily Post.* The kind where it looks like you have got a giant foot. (I had a hole in my pumps).

Stoke-on Trent was next, and then back to Manchester. In between, I visited ladies at home who had been in hospital. I was still in close touch with the group members although we had not resumed group meetings. This was mainly because some were still having treatment. Some wanted to get back to normal family life and weren't able to while group meetings reminded them of their pain and worry. This was fine by me. The group was still there for people who had a need and the idea to me of a good group is finding at the end of the day, that the person no longer needs to come, they can manage themselves. This is the idea of self-help. A shoulder to lean on when needed, and goodbye, when the need no longer exists, leaving room for new members. I am flattered to say that all members keep in touch with me, and I'm talking about a thousand or so women just here in Liverpool, not counting ladies who wrote or telephoned, or ladies from other cities. What a wonderful feeling of sistership!

I gave talks to private establishments who train young people and Y.T.S. places of training. I visited cancer care homes, and women meeting in groups in their own homes. I spoke to welfare groups, attended 'lingerie parties' and fortune-telling parties.

I spoke at under/post graduate medical meetings and went to friend's christening 'do's'. I never had time to get bored, that was for sure. The work was varied and very interesting. The only time I dreaded a visit, was when I knew it was a person who was going to die. I felt privileged and really special, that a person would want to spend time with me at this sad part of their lives, because most of them knew they were going to die. Yes, even where a kindly, well-meaning relative had kept the news from the persons, that person knew, some inner instinct perhaps. The liked talking to me because they didn't have to pretend. They could say what they wanted. I promised the confidentiality and that is exactly what they got. I often found that in that sort of situation, the dying person wouldn't talk about it for fear of upsetting the family, and family wouldn't talk about for the same reason. Yet each knew that the other knew. It was their way of handling it. I say I dreaded it, because each time I was present, I mourned, and felt upset. Each time I cried, and each time I wanted to bang my head against the wall and shout out *why*! I also asked why in my relationship with Chris, why weren't things getting better? They were definitely getting worse. We couldn't stay in the same room these days without picking at each other and often this developed into a full blown argument. We never used to be like this. Oh, we'd have tiffs, maybe fall out over something silly, but that was easily solved when we got to bed, toes across the mattress, stray fingers touching and the quarrel was soon forgotten. But not now. The simplest row went on for days, usually with one of us sleeping down stairs. I couldn't take much more, I had to get away. I wouldn't have thought of actually leaving home, of course. There were the kids to think about. One day things got so bad, I walked out of the house and went walking through the nearby cemetery. My mum and Chris's mum are buried there, I walked between the graves, deep in thought. I stopped by mum's grave where I sat down and lit a cigarette. I often did this when I wanted to think. I tried to rationalise the whole situation and our life together, if that's what you would call it. I tried to put myself in his place. How would I feel if my once loving wife suddenly stopped being loving at all? I realised that I would not like it. I would probably be angry and suspicious. Did she have a new lover? Was it her age as the doctor said? I could understand how he must feel. That did not help me at all to come to terms with my reactions to my dilemma, I decided we would make love that night whether it hurt or not. Maybe it was all in the mind, we'd try!

We did, and it hurt like hell. It was certainly not in my mind, because the pain continued for two days after. Anyway, I'm not the type to imagine things, and I did so want my married life to return to normal, if I could remember what normal was.

What was I supposed to do? Make love every night even though it hurt. NO! to hell with that. Love was meant to be pleasant not painful! I wasn't prepared to suffer every night just so that he could have his satisfaction. If he really loved me, he wouldn't want to cause me pain, he would be more understanding. I said as much to him.
He replied: "Well I know, but I can't help myself."
I got fed up asking the doctor why I was having painful sex. I have never to this day, got a reasonable reply.
"It shouldn't hurt", "Are you worrying too much?" were some of the answers I got. In other words, they simply didn't know, or they weren't going to tell me if they did, because I was suing the authority?
I was angry all right. Not only at the state of the system, but with the state of my marriage. I knew quite a few of the other women were suffering in a similar way. I suppose on that score, I should consider myself 'lucky'. At least Chris didn't physically abuse me, and I had heard of one or two cases where the husband had hurt his wife.
Chris and I were holding on. I think for the sake of the good years we had, we were both hoping that one day, things would get better, if only we could hold on. Many a time, he has been on the point of packing his bags and going, and many times, I felt like telling him to, but something holds us back from severing that final thread. Let's hope that thread is very strong, and can keep us together until, somehow, this thing sorts itself out.
I felt sorry for Chris in ways. I had my work, I could bury myself in it when things got too much. Chris has no real hobbies, apart from his music, which he plays a lot these

days. Music, however doesn't occupy the mind the way study does, so I suppose, his mind still wanders.
The year is almost over and I am no nearer to seeing the full report than I was in September last year. I am going to take some drastic action. I will not be stifled. I had to have the truth. I had to find a way of gaining some strong support, and so I decided to write to every Member of Parliament in the country, every single one. I am told M.P.'s do not usually reply to 'circular type' letters and yet I cannot afford to write individual letters to all 600 odd of them. It would be quite expensive to send out circulars, and I would have to deliver them by hand because I can't afford the postage, so I had to take the chance.
It was indeed a mammoth task. I composed a letter on one side of an A4 sheet.
I obtained a list with the names of all M.P.'s from a friend in London and set about addressing the envelopes. My two eldest daughters, a couple of their friends and a neighbour helped put the letters into the envelopes and then came the worst part of all. Licking the damned things. We had sore tongues for weeks, but we did it.
By chance, around that time, I ran into Sylvia Sharpey-Schafer, a councillor I had met at the womens Labour Movement meeting. When I told her of my intentions, she said that Terry Fields M.P. was in Liverpool, and he would be happy to deliver the letters for me when he returned to the House of Commons in two days. That would suit me very well, just enough time, and how it would save me.
December, 13th., unlucky for some, but not for me. This was the day I had arranged with Sylvia to meet Terry Fields at the Town Hall with the letters. The press were there, and some photographs were taken. The photographer took the picture of Terry, Sylvia and me handing over the letters

outside the Town Hall, but when it appeared in the papers next day, they only showed me. Something to do with elections. They didn't want to be seen to be taking sides I suppose. It didn't bother me that it was a politician who was helping me, nor did I mind what party he represented. I would have been grateful to any M.P. who had offered to help in this. I was still not politically minded, nor did I belong to any particular party. I was not in the least bit interested in that sort of thing. The same evening, the CHC held their AGM for 1988. I was not asked to speak at this but I was present, and I had written an article for the Annual Report, up-dating members on my campaign efforts and the effects of the system on women's lives.

I also wrote a long detailed letter to Mrs. Thatcher, the Prime Minister at that time.

I am not too sure what I expected to gain by writing to the M.P.'s. I didn't really expect a different response from the Prime Minister, but I felt she should know the strength of our feelings, and that we would not let the matter rest.

Imagine the surprise, when on 23rd December, I received my first replies from M.P.'s, 14 in all. I didn't expect to hear so quickly. Some were postcards acknowledging my letter and promising to report in due course, and some had actually written giving me their support. They were from various parties, but all were represented. All party leaders wrote to me except the leader of the Labour party. He must have been too busy??

It was after the Christmas holidays that most of the replies were received, over twenty per cent had responded. I am told that this was excellent.

Sadly, although the response was very good and I received some really nice letters, it had little bearing on the object in sight. The Health Authority Chairman said to the press that he was not prepared to even discuss the possibility of disclosing the full report. So although my attempts were futile, I had to try. I kept on trying over the years, and even when another recall woman died just before Christmas 1990, they still would not release that ruddy report. One must wonder what it contained that it needed to be guarded so much.

1989 began peacefully enough. Lunch with Helen and Margaret, a visit to a woman in hospital, a visit to a health centre, and then my own check-up visit to the Royal Liverpool hospital.

Our group had started meeting again, with mostly new members. The 'old' members called in occasionally. Fundraising continued and by March, I was looking to start another group in the Huyton area. I was still travelling. I had been to Accrington and was about to go to London for the second time this year, to meet with Jan who was in the process of forming an 'Association' of some kind. I began to have dealings with the Eastern CHC. At this time, I was training a young lady called Debbie Conway, who was going to be group leader in the area, and I took her along to introduce her to Frank Rose, the Chief officer and his assistant Audrey. Many of Debbie's prospective clients would be in their area, and so I wanted her to see the wealth of information which was available at CHC offices. When I first met Frank, he was wary of me I think, but he later told me he had become accustomed to me "plodding along" as he called it, and I can safely say that we three have become pretty good friends. I often ring Frank and Audrey for 'little favours.'

The year wore on and I was collecting new clients at quite a rate. The group had spread its wings and we now covered things like breast screening/womens general problems. The little old self-help group was fast becoming an 'organisation'. These days, I'm up and down to London

like a yo yo. I was thinking of pitching a tent in Trafalgar Square. We are fast heading for 1990, and Jan has asked me to speak at the Inaugural Meeting of her association.
Now this really was important. At last I would get to meet the people behind the laboratory walls, the faceless ones in their white coats. I didn't mean that as a criticism of laboratory staff, as I have already said, they saved my life. But if I could reach them and make them see how we women felt when someone gets it wrong, maybe, if I could let them share our pain then perhaps they would do something, influence someone - anything to stop the pain and 'carnage' of female lives. Surprise, surprise, they were very human, very sympathetic, and they shared my concern. They were anxious to produced a better system, and to change things for the better all round. I already suspected they would be like this because I had carried out my own private 'survey' of client cases and discovered that less than 20% of all errors were lab errors and in the remaining cases the problem was medical in the sense that women found it quite difficult to get their G.P. to refer them to the hospital clinic. Most women who consulted their G.P., if they were without physical symptoms, were treated as 'it's all in the mind' cases. There were also a strange 'rivalry' between Cytology and Colposcopy. I would have thought that one should complement the other, but in many cases, not so, and sometimes with disastrous results.
I do not have space here to tell you all that went on that day, although I would love to, but suffice to say I shared the platform with some very distinguished people from the world of medicine and histopathology. I was so very pleased that I was able to speak to such a good mixture of people who were directly involved with smear testing, and I did reach them. Many came to me after the meeting and told me I had brought tears to their eyes. I had succeeded. I

had made them feel some of our pain. Would it do any good? I believe it has, because I am now on first name terms with many on the inside, and they are surprisingly open with me. I would feel able to contact them if I felt there was a problem. I could ask for advice, and know that they would be truthful with me.

May, 1990, I was to have an exploratory operation. I was still having pains and there had been some unexplained bleeding, but thankfully, this showed that there were no more cancer cells present. Sadly, my Father-in-Law John (Chris) passed away so I cancelled my appointments for the week. I got on very well with him and I would miss him. He was a nice person, and caring. I felt depressed after the funeral and once again, I was glad of my work.

This year had been even busier than those proceeding years, probably because I was becoming more well known, with more people contacting me. This was good.

Strange, I have written many thousands of words and yet I have only touched the edge of the whole story. I regret what I have had to omit but it would have been impossible to include all the events and name all the people I had been in contact with during these four years. I have only touched on my personal life. There has been so much pain, sadness and regrets. I must now accept I will never be the same woman I was before the cancer blunder. I feel that I have been robbed of four years in my life, and like all time, when it has passed, it can never be recalled.

If time could not be recalled in my life, neither could it be recalled in the lives of my children.

Little Chrissie was four years old when this thing began, and still very much a baby. I turn around, and she's fast approaching nine. Where did my baby go? I can't even remember her first day at the 'big school'. What was her teacher's name? Who were her little friends? Did I visit her school during that first year, if so, for what reason? Has it all faded in the mists of time, or was I too busy in other directions? I can clearly remember the first day at school of my other four children. Liz cried, and took quite some time to settle, while Julie went in, holding the hand of her teacher, smiling and content, looking back at me and waving. It was me who cried that day. Dainty little shy Nickie, oh how she cried, the Headmistress had to take her into her office. I later discovered that dear lady had 'bribed' her with orange juice and a biscuit. It took Nickie over a week to settle. Jamie, like the little man he was, marched boldy into school, not a care in the world and settled right away. Talking about Jamie, he was nine when my health problem began, and was quite the little 'tough guy'. He had been rather too quiet as a toddler, but we needn't have worried. Suddenly when he was four, he told us he wanted to go to morning nursery at the local school. He couldn't wait to start at 'big school'. I look around at him now, he is no longer a child. Somewhere I have missed the transformation. He is taller than me and takes a size eight shoe, the same size as his dad. When did he start to change? Or was it so gradual that I didn't notice? That is a sad and disagreeable thing to have to admit to. Nichola, twelve at the start, came in one day wearing make-up. As I was about to reprimand her, I stopped, realising in a flash as it were, that she was sixteen years old. How and when had that happened? Somewhere along the line, Julie had left home and was now in teacher training college. Was that because of the blunder? Why did she go? Should I have taken more interest? I just don't know! Liz, as you know had already left home prior to the blunder. I am left with a tremendous feeling of guilt. Why did it happen? When did it happen? I really cannot answer. The children were never neglected, nothing like that. They had a warm, clean bed, enough clothing, enough food. They were never left alone. There was always a responsible adult with them when I was out, but that was not enough, they were deprived of their mother. They witnessed arguments between their parents. Not the silly rows we used to have, rows that made the kids laugh at us next day, but serious rows. They were there to watch their parents drift apart. Change from 'loving silly billies', to people with almost hate in their eyes. They must also have heard our rows in the bedroom. How embarrassing, to think that the children are listening to our arguments about sex.

When Liz was at home, the summer before the blunder, it was a very different story. Chris and I were like Romeo and Juliet, we were always 'at it!' What was it Liz used to say when she caught us 'together' (and I don't mean she actually seen us making love!) canoodling? "I seen that! I heard that!" We would giggle like a couple of kids and the other children would join in chanting the same words. We would all laugh, happy laughter, as a family. Even when we had a tiff, the kids would just shrug and grin, because they knew it won't be long before we made up, and then it would be 'giggling time' again.

We were pleased and proud that our children could react in this way to the canoodlings of their parents, because so few parents are able to express their feelings for each other in front of their children, but those days have gone for good it would appear. The blunder had not only affected my cervix, it had affected my whole being and every fibre of my family life.

It made me very angry when those in authority claimed that we had not suffered any additional stress as a result of the blunder. They claimed that any woman who had an abnormal smear would suffer the same. Well, I know lots of women who have had an abnormal smear and although they were naturally worried for a time, they were able to settle down quite happily after they had been treated and cleared. With the recall women, it was bad enough finding out we were clear, but finding out from the media, I don't think anyone would be able to understand how devastated we were, unless they had been directly involved with us.

How I mourned those lost years, I longed to be the happy-go-lucky sex-mad wife. I even longed for the silly quarrels we used to have mainly caused by the pressures of life on the dole. I know that we both feel the same. Not that we have actually talked about it, we seldom actually talk at all these days. How can I get rid of this feeling of resentment? God knows I've tried. I have lost count of the times I have planned an alluring return to our sex life. The full works, sexy nightie, soft lights, sweet-smelling bath, everything you could think of, and then, crossed words, the end of another lovely dream, or he would make a grab at 'those bits'. I find that a great big 'turn-off'. I am a whole person. I want to be made love to, I am not a vessel for male satisfaction. I suppose in reality, the poor sod had been deprived so much, he was desperate. Maybe I shouldn't talk like that about my husband, but it's probably true. It is no more his fault than is it mine. We are caught in a trap and we can't get out. Too late for sex therapy, although this may have helped in the beginning. No, we will have to find our own way. I still love him, and I know he still loves me, but resentment is a great passion killer. That will have to go before we resume any kind of meaningful relationship. But How?

Chapter 14

KILROY

Funnily enough, although we suffered from resentment and debilitation in our private life, it did not spill over into my public life.

In this Chris was very supportive. He did all he could to help. For example, if I was appearing on T.V. or on the radio, he would carefully record the programme. He took telephone calls when I was out. As a rule one of the girls would do this, but when we were all out Chris was there. He was proud of me and my efforts. I know this from the way he spoke to people about me. It was strange. It was as though we were two different people. One personality in public and a different one in private. If the T.V. people were filming in our home, he would either stay out of the way, or make the tea. He supported me every step of my campaign. Like the time I was asked to appear on the *Kilroy* show. He was very pleased about that. We both were, because that particular show had the reputation of being open and controversial. Apparently, a group from the London area, a newish womens group, had come up with the following suggestion - that women should withold their sexual favours to their partners, unless he came up with £5.00, to be sent to the said group. Someone from the Kilroy team rang me, and asked for my reaction to this. Of course I was furious. Here we were trying so hard to get rid of the 'promiscuity' label so how would it sound if we began charging our partners for sex? I was sure the group were well-intentioned, but really, I ask you, I certainly did not approve of their methods.

I was asked to appear on the show I think, as a rabble-rouser. For the first time I was happy to live up to this title. I readily agreed. I would have to ring Betty and James in Glasgow. How many times had Betty said that she would like to see me on the *Kilroy* show. She was going to get her wish.

I was also asked to bring with me some women who had had an abnormal smear, or who had suffered as a result of bad practice in our hospital. There was no shortage of women who fitted into this category, but I wanted to try to high-light different kinds of cases. Eventually, I decided to ask Lynn from Glasgow, who had been kept waiting for her laser treatment in a hospital corridor, and who received her treatment in a room she describes as a 'broom cupboard'. I also took Susan from Liverpool, who had needed a hysterectomy as a result, directly or indirectly, of the blunder. Another lady from Liverpool was my third choice. Joan, who had a history in her family of cancer, and who was being kept waiting rather too long to be comfortable. She was extremely worried.

Chris was very helpful that day, taking charge of the children and the house while I made the necessary phone calls and arrangements.

The three of us travelled to London by train. We had arranged to meet Lynn at Euston Station.

When we arrived at the studios we were given seat numbers. Those who occupied the front seats were supplied with a little microphone. Guess who was one of them?

We were given refreshments in a sort of ante-room before going into the studio. There was plenty of time for discussions, which were very enlightening. We women brought our chairs into a circle. Some were health workers, others were women who had been affected in some way by the system. The professional guests stuck together. I'm sure this was not intentional, it was just that they knew each other. We had been told that Edwina Currie had been invited but was unable to come. I wonder why? Another minister would take her place. Damn, I thought. I would love to have got Edwina on this show. I had a few words to say to that lady.

The show began with Kilroy speaking to the group leader. She told the viewers of her intention and when challenged about the implications, she said that it wasn't meant to be offensive, and I'm sure she meant it. I thought she was just a middle-class, misguided woman. Perhaps I am not being fair, because her idea had worked. Her plans had drawn attention to the plight of women with problems, and our present day system for womens' health.

Anyway, the conversation got around to promiscuity as I knew it was bound to with this topic. I simply had to butt in. I wasn't going to listen to all the rubbish about promiscuous women.

I said they should be testing men if men were the source, and that testing women was rather like bolting the stable door after the horse had bolted. I would maintain that claim to this day. If they had not discovered that the 'wart virus' was not quite the cause, it was supposed to be in the development of cervical cancer.

The wart virus, you see, was said to be a sexually transmitted disease, and so by implication, if it indeed went on to cause cervical cancer, then that disease could also be called sexually transmitted. They have apparently and recently discovered that perhaps the wart virus is not quite the 'bogey man' they once thought. This is because in these studies, it appears that the wart virus is everywhere. Up our noses, in our tubes, on our hands, in fact, everywhere you might find a 'common or garden' wart, you could also find the dreaded Human Papilloma-Virus.

The women were well satisfied with the end product. We felt we had supported our 'side' as much as we could, given that, as must be normal on such a show, time ran out.

A light buffet was provided for us after the show, and again we had the opportunity to mix and chat. I made some very useful contacts there, and am still in touch with some of the women even now.

For those of you who have not met Robert Kilroy Silk. He is every inch, the handsome, successful T.V. presenter, and is also, I'm sure a very good businessman. Underneath that carefully kept exterior, I believe he is a very sincere person. He looked after me well. He escorted me around the various groups of people introducing me to people who might be able to help me in some way, or where I might be able to engage in arguing a point or two. I was ever ready to do this. He had no need to take an interest in me now the show was over, the cameras gone. I talked with him at some length and I liked the man, not because he was good-looking, but because I felt he is a nice person.

See what I mean about people taking an interest. It felt good, and these people had nothing to gain. If I had been a young girl, then there are those who might think there was an ulterior motive, but with my formidable reputation, and the fact that I am not so young, only serve to show that these people were sincere. I should also point out that I am not the sort of person who is flattered by the attention of the famous. I long ago realised that even the famous are only human. I have met in my travels many famous people, and you will notice that I am not praising too many of them. Speaks for itself doesn't it. Not that I'm criticising those who did not try to help. I suppose they thought that it wasn't their affair.

Chris was very pleased with my efforts on the *Kilroy* show. He had recorded it well. I was quite surprised at the way I came over. I hadn't realised that I would seem so aggressive. I felt that way, but as I have said before, sometimes it doesn't come out the way we might intend. This show certainly did. Lynn and 'Susan' both got some very good points across, and it is quite difficult to get a word in edgeways on this type of show. Joan didn't manage to say anything, but we were very pleased that she was with us. It showed our strength to appear together. We certainly had lots to talk about on our journey home. Lynn stayed in London as she had arranged to meet a friend.

Many little things happened away from the public eye, but which are very important to me. For example, nice little thank-you cards from ladies I had helped. Now there is nothing greater than the words 'thank-you', especially when you know they are sincere. I have kept every one of these cards. I wouldn't part with them for the world. I have also received letters of thanks, such lovely letters it makes me feel like crying. These letters and cards are very much a part of the whole issue. It is a wonderful feeling to have helped someone, and even greater to hear them say so. When people ask me why I do what I do, I tell you now, this is why. This feeling is better than all the tea in China. I know you can't live on good feelings and probably one day I will seek paid employment, but it will have to fit in with my group work. I have put too much into this work to just drop it now, and to be truthful, I don't really want to drop it. I love what I'm doing. I get more satisfaction now than when I was earning wages.

One day when the system is working well there will be no more need for people like me. I will be quite happy to 'retire'. Maybe write my 'Jesus Book', who knows, but not yet!

Chapter 15

JUSTICE

Although justice has prevailed, in that we had been granted legal aid, we were still a long way from reaching the courts.
Our solicitors had to find medical experts who were prepared to support our claim for damages, in person, if necessary. There were not too many of those around. Some experts made wishy-washy statements, others were down right hostile claiming that we had not suffered as a result of the blunder, or the delay in treatment.
We had collected thousands of pages of medical studies to support our claim, and to be fair, we had included material for and against us. There were a reasonable amount of studies which suggested that delay in treatment did put women at greater risk, and also stated that additional treatments can be required if there is such a delay.
We presented some of these documents to the 'hostile' experts, and although there was material which had been written by that expert, they were going against their own written word. I couldn't believe it, these people made me sick! When we pointed out to them, that they, themselves had written some of the material, they were still not prepared to agree with us, making various excuses, such as....''Opinions vary''....''Times have changed''....''Certain treatments/tests were not available in certain areas''....''At the time when it occurred''....''different now''.
These were the people who were supposed to be looking after us! They couldn't even agree with themselves.
We eventually had to go out of the country to find experts

who would give us a fair opinion. It was a mammoth task, because you see, we not only needed Cytological, Histopathelogical, and Gynaecological evidence, we also needed Psychiatric evidence, as we had suffered emotional and mental trauma as a result of the whole fiasco.

In my opinion, even the 'legal treatment' received by some of the women was grossly unfair. In those days, solicitors were not allowed to advertise their speciality, unlike doctors I might add, and so women were going to solicitors who had very little experience of medical negligence matters. This is not a criticism of solicitors by the way, but there were some cases which I believe were handled rather poorly, which leaves me feeling that the law governing medical negligence cases is well over-due for change. Even solicitors who are very experienced in medical negligence have difficulties proving a case, so how can we expect solicitors who are experienced only in the general law to cope. Incidently, it is interesting to note that of all who go to litigation regarding a medical negligence claim, very few actually reach the courts, and of those who do, very few win their case. It is not enough to prove how much you have suffered, an almost impossible task. It is wrong that a health authority is allowed to admit that a "massive error of professional judgement" has occurred, then in the next breath say that they do not admit liability.

Then, as though to add insult to injury, the Health Authority made an offer to certain of the women. Originally, it seemed to me that was those who had suffered least, as in the opinion of the Authority, some would have needed the same treatment even if they had been recalled at the correct time and so they had only suffered trauma etc., but not so, as the cases were all very different.

I recall at the beginning of this 'mix-up', the authorities were asked, probably by some of our legal representatives, to make an out of court offer. They replied that they could not, as each case would have to be judged on its own merits. It would appear that it now suited them to change their minds. Perhaps we had become a 'nuisance', or maybe they wanted this mess cleared up before the 'opting out' got underway. Who knows, or is telling?

I cannot be precise about the figures, but I understand the individual offers made were £350, to £750, neither can I tell you exactly how many women received these offers as many dropped their legal cases, perhaps because they were told that they didn't 'have a case'. There were many reasons. I was quoted at the time as saying "I was pleased that an offer had been made, and although it was rather low, it was a start."

I was pleased that negotiations had at last been opened, but I felt that the women deserved a much better deal than that which had been made. Most solicitors, I understand, were prepared to advise their clients that, as the offer was low, it might be in their best interest to refuse, but I believe some ladies accepted this first figure. I really can understand why they would be tempted to take the offer. They had been through the mill, medically and legally, and just wanted to forget what had happened and get on with their lives. There were certain people with 'political leanings' who tried to persuade the women to hold out for a much higher figure, not from a specific party because there was more than one involved. I thought this was out of order and I said so on the Johnny Kennedy Show. These women had suffered enough and it was most unfair to put them under further pressure.

I, more than anybody should have wanted them to hold out. It would have been more prestigious for my campaign, the higher the number, you know! But I refused to put pressure on them. No campaign is worth a persons emotional or psychological well- being.

I told the women who contacted me that they should think very carefully about the offer, have a chat with their solicitor, and then if they wished, they should accept.

A second offer was made at a later date. This was slightly higher, ranging from £500 to £950 approximately, and a few more ladies accepted this. Quite a few still refused, feeling that the offers were insultingly low after what they had been through. I back all of the ladies all of the way. Whatever they choose to do, they must be allowed to make the choice they believe is best and right for them. They have had little choice in anything else that has happened to them since this 'thing' began.

Interestingly enough, round about the time when the first offers were made, a man was in the news having accepted an offer of £10,000 for a failed vasectomy. Now of course this man deserved his compensation, but didn't we? Who had been kept waiting for three and a half years at the time. There were also many famous people in news having received very large sums of money for libel/slanderous 'assaults' on their character. Is it any wonder that we felt slighted by this pittance disguised as an offer of compensation?

Chapter 16

BLUNDER REPORT

The Internal Review Report.

Now that is a document to be reckoned with. This very abridged version in its pale blue cover began with pages one and two which contained the *SUMMARY OF REPORT* as follows:-
1. Between March 1983 and December 1985, 45,000 smears were processed at the Womens' Hospital.
2. After checks, it was necessary to review 911 slides, and to recall 487 women for further checks.
3. The abnormalities were first suspected by Laboratory staff.
4. The staff tried to draw attention to their concerns.
5. The scale of the "missed tests is very large", and can only be described as "a massive error of professional judgement for which we can offer no logical explaination".
6. We are satisfied that the action instituted by Dr. P.A. Smith was correct.
7. Management arrangements covering the Labs were very weak.
8. The conduct of the laboratory staff cannot be criticised.
9. A more rigorous system of quality control could have reduced the problem.
Obviously, the above nine conclusions have been further abbreviated by me, but the general context is there.
We now find that the report jumps to page twenty-three, and ends with page twenty-seven. These pages are filled

with the conclusions of the panel, and their recommendations.
It mentions that the arrangements for Locum Consultants appointments were not complied with, and questions the age limit of 70 years for such people. It takes into consideration the opinion of the outside experts that the slides were "described as being beyond any possible doubt". It then goes on to discuss an allegation of "switching", and expresses disappointment that this allegation was made. Talks about the Administrative Consultant who did nothing when approached and names another doctor who was approached by the lab staff, and who also did nothing claiming that he felt unable to question a colleague about the quality of their work. Again it states that the lab staff could not be blamed, that only Dr. Smith can be commended, and finally that the recall arrangements were handled with "commendable thoroughness". I see no point in going into the recommendations which occupy pages twenty-six and seven, because these are not in dispute. As far as I am concerned, the whole procedure was a complete waste of time, and an insult to our intelligence. It told us little we did'nt already know from the dilligence of our newspaper reporter Steve Harrison. He had told us as much as they had.
What I wanted to know was why they found it necessary to exclude pages three to twenty-two inclusive from this document. Their reply was that they were unable to publish witnesses testimonies.
I told the public I was not satisfied with this version of the report, and I meant that. As you know, I campaigned for a full public inquiry, backed by the CHC and others. I requested sight of the full report, but to no avail. They were guarding their full package of secrets well, locked up in a safe at Health Authority Headquarters, but why? What

was so damning about the witnesses testimonies that they had to be hidden from the public? I would certainly not rest until I found out.

Due to my poking and prodding in recent months I found a 'source' who shall remain nameless, who was prepared to allow me brief access to a less abridged version of the report. I cannot go into detail to preserve the person's identity.

I sat down at the desk with the document, feeling strangely calm. The person left the room as they wanted as little involvement with this exercise as possible, saying they would return in about fifteen minutes. In other words, that is the time I was going to be allowed. I was not able to ask questions nor discuss the report. It was left on the desk and I was left alone with it. I thought: "That will do nicely".

I quickly read through the pages, mostly containing witnesses testimonies. I must make notes. Fortunately I am a quick writer and I'm quick to understand the written word. I was able to copy from all relevent pages, and finished just as my source returned. I quickly thanked them and left. I couldn't wait to get home to study my notes. I had made doubly sure to take notes of names of witnesses and of those present at the review. I double checked my notes for accuracy.

OK, lets look at the evidence.

It begins by saying that Dr. P. Smith reported to Dr. J. Philips that there was a problem on 16th. December 1986. He had checked the index cards and if the difference between the screener and the pathologist was significant, then he re-examined the actual slide.

It was noted that there was "a loss of confidence among the women of Merseyside".

After consulting with the Merseyside Regional Health Authority, and the Department of Health and Social Security, it was decided to hold an Internal Review.

Dr. Lodge.

Dr. Kathleen Lodge was offered the appointment of Locum Consultant at the Womens' Hospital for two sessions per week, later increased to three. Dr. Jones stated he did not recommend Dr. Lodge to Dr. Philips, but merely mentioned her name (as a retired consultant). No check was made on Dr. Lodge's suitability for the post. Dr. Philips had assumed this had been done. It was assumed Dr. Lodge's past experience as Senior Consultant in the North West Region was sufficient evidence of her competence. *No* references were sought or obtained. Dr. Philips saw no problem during Dr. Lodge's term of employment. Dr. Lodge was actually asked to stay on for a further three months until Dr. Smith took over in December '85.

Dr. Jones

Dr. Jones stated that he did not attempt to judge the work done by the consultant, he only looked after staffing levels. He engaged in other work outside the Womens'. He was budget holder for Pathology at the Womens', St. Pauls, Sefton General and the Maternity Hospital.

He did not accept responsibility for work, but rather expected staff to stand on their own feet.

It is stated that the last locum at the Women's Hospital was Dr. J. Vickers, and that Dr. Lodge's husband is Dr. Woodcock, a pathologist at the Royal Hospital. Dr. Philips is adamant that Dr. Jones recommended Dr. Lodge. Dr. Jones again denies this.

The "review is satisfied that Dr. Jones acted in good faith."

Laboratory staff stress that they tried to bring the matter up with Dr. Jones he also denies this. When asked what he would have done had he been aware of the problem, he says that he would have spoken to Dr. Lodge.
"The review is satisfied that Dr. Jones was approached, but failed to comprehend the scale of the problem. He took no action".

Dr. P. Smith
Appointed in July 1985 to do six sessions as Histopathologist and Cytopathologist at R.L.H. in the University Department and five sessions at the Women's Hospital.
From July to September (approx.) Dr. Smith worked with Dr. Lodge. He noticed that staff had difficulties and had little confidence in Dr. Lodge. He and Dr. Lodge had widely different views on screening, so much so that he sent a sample to Dr. Hussein at Charing Cross Hospital in London for his opinion. Dr. Hussein agreed with Dr. Smith. Dr. Smith then went to a training session at the Western Infirmary in Glasgow. On his return Dr. Mc.Dicken, (a senior lecturer and Honorary Consultant L.H.A.) informed him that the technicians had shown him a number of cases which had been screened by them as abnormal and which had been passed by Dr. Lodge as normal. Dr. Mc.Dicken said to Dr. Smith that a direct approach to Dr. Lodge was out of the question, but he agreed with the technicians. (It is further noted by the review, that G.P.s or Consultants did not question the strange behaviour of the technicians who took it upon themselves to send some cases for repeat smears in three to six months).
Repeat smears began to arrive over the following months and Dr. Smith was dismayed at the number of cases involved. When he reviewed the original slides, every one

showed significant abnormalities. By April 1986, there were at least fifty cases. Dr. Smith was by now convinced that something had gone very wrong throughout Dr. Lodge's appointment. The discrepancies between Dr. Lodge and the technicians were so striking that he believed that they were far beyond the scope of simple errors of judgement. The word 'incompetence' was used here.

Dr. Smith approached the Medical Defence Union and was advised by them to inform the Authority in December 1986.

45,000 files were searched for 1983-84-85. This identified 929 slides which had been reported as negative, were in fact not negative.

(At this point in the enquiry, Pearse Butler questioned the figure of 929, saying that he had not seen this version, and knew only of 911, but that he would look into it).

Which ever figure was correct, half were sent to Dr. Hussein in London, and half to Dr. D.M.D. Evans in Cardiff for re- assessment. Both agreed with Dr. Smith's diagnosis. When asked why it took him so long to report the matter, Dr. Smith stated that he was unsure how many were involved and wanted to keep things in perspective. Eventually, 487 patients were recalled for "Physical Examination".

In November 1985, Dr. McDicken was approached by a senior MLSO, who informed him of the problem. He suggested that the patients should be recalled but that they should wait until Dr. Smith returned from Glasgow. Dr. McDicken stated to the review, that he does not recall being approached by this MLSO, nor does he recall being approached by two other senior technicians at an earlier date. He was also asked to bring the matter up with Dr. Jones, but said that "Dr. Jones made relatively few appearances at the Womens". The board were satisfied that Dr. McDicken could not cope, and that he had been

approached more than once, but that he was unlikely to have done anything positive.
Evidence follows from five senior members of the laboratory staff. They all became aware of the discrepancies soon after Dr. Lodge's appointment in March 1983. The Senior Chief MLSO approached Dr. Lodge directly but with no success. Dr. Jones made no approach to Dr. Lodge but suggested that her judgement was on the conservative side. He took no action and the report states that if he had, he could have limited the problem.
Dr. Lodge reviewed a sample of the suspect slides and confirmed, and agreed with the outside experts' opinion. She states that she could not have made mistakes of this kind because of her experience and knowledge of cytopathology, it was inconceivable. A question was put to Dr. Lodge by a member of the review. Dr. Lodge states that she was confident she had not seen the slides before, but that she did not wish to make any accusations or insinuations. Question put to Dr. Lodge by a second member: "Did she at any time feel the volume of work pressure?"
she replied, "Not at all, not in any way".
The report then states that the suggestion by Dr. Lodge's legal representative, of the possibility of 'switching' of slides is far more serious.
So serious in fact, that three members of the review visited the laboratory to investigate the allegations. As a result of their visit it was stated that the allegations were "not substantiated" and must be dismissed with a degree of disappointment that they were raised in the first place.
The review team could offer no reasonable explaination as to why the obvious and correct diagnosis was not made.
Next, there was the evidence of Professor H. Fox, who examined fifty-two cases with colleagues. He agreed with

the outside experts and stated that in forty-four of these cases, the slides required little more than a glance.

I have given you a brief synopsis of both reports. I can assure you that I have not omitted any important or leading information.

I will now tell you what I believe may have happened based on the reports, on verbal information which has come my way, and on my own first hand involvement/knowledge of the fiasco, which was 'lovingly' called a 'mix-up'.

Firstly we have the various levels of 'debate'. The 'he did, she did, I did, you did', parts followed by the 'did'nt feel able to approach a colleague', 'Let's wait until he returns'. In other words, lets pass the buck!

Don't you think that this was disgraceful behaviour seeing that the lives of nearly 1,000 women may have been at stake? No, I am not trying to 'exaggerate' the matter, nor am I trying to make it just sound worse. I don't have to do that! They did a very good job of making the matter sound worse when they attempted what was commonly known as a 'cover-up'.

The sad fact is 487 women had to be urgently recalled for physical examination because their reviewed smears were very abnormal, suggesting that lives may well have been in danger, and the remaining 400 or so may only have been safe because of the 'illegal' actions of the laboratory staff. What we are left with is absolute carelessness, and diabolical *COMPLACENCY!*

Let us not forget that but for 58 'missing ladies' (women who the authorities failed to trace because they had moved, etc.) we may never have known about the blunder. I was recalled twice to the Women's, and once to The Royal Liverpool Hospital for tests and results prior to treatment and no-one in authority told me that something was wrong. None of the recalled women have ever been told, officially,

that 'something' had gone wrong, and so I feel we are justified in stating that there was an attempted cover-up.
Secondly we should seriously think about the allegation of 'switching'. It is pointless the Authority saying that they were 'disappointed'. It was raised, and it is useless them saying that an investigation was carried out if they will not say how this was done.
How could they investigate such an allegation? Switching means exactly that. A person or persons switching the positive slides which may have been left for Dr. Lodge to examine for negative ones, and then after assessment, switching the originals back again. I agree with the Authority on one thing. It is a very serious allegation, and one which would have been practically impossible to investigate. And so, when the Authority stated that the allegation was not substantiated, we must assume they meant that they could find no proof.
As you know, I have visited that very laboratory, and I have spoken to many people about lab workings in general. As a result, I find it entirely believable that 'switching' could have occurred. The evidence offered to the inquiry clearly states that health professionals find it more or less impossible to approach or reproach a colleague regarding their work, and so it is also believable that a 'person in a white coat' could have used the lab to obtain samples for their own 'clinical trials' or 'studies' without being asked to explain their actions.
The very fact that the allegation was raised by Dr. Lodge's legal representative implies that she discussed the matter with him, and although she states that she felt unable to make accusations, perhaps he thought that in order to make fair representation on behalf of his client then he should raise the subject.

It would now be reasonable for you to ask: ''Why switch slides, and to what purpose?''
Well, we may never know whether or not switching occurred, and we may never know the true reason for switching if indeed it did occur. But as an example, we could look again at the 'New Zealand Experiment', where a 'white-coated god' witheld treatment, almost on a 'whim' to prove his point. He was of course a 'big noise' in his country, and as such, could 'rule the roost', but what if a 'smaller fry' wanted to prove a point? They could switch the positive slides for negatives, so that the patient would not be given treatment, thus achieving their objective without anyone knowing, and effectively, 'witholding' treatment. This is just one possible example of why switching might be useful. There are many others. The allegation is therefore, a very serious one to raise, and I'll admit that I too am surprised and concerned that it was. While it is most unlikely that proof will ever be found to substantiate the allegation, there is the old saying which might be appropriate, 'there's no smoke without fire!'
This is merely supposition about the Liverpool incident. The New Zealand affair is quite different. I feel quite confident in discussing this because I have the necessary proof in my hand. I have a copy of the *metro* magazine article which sparked off the inquiry, several newspaper cuttings, plus a copy of the Public Inquiry Transcript lead by Judge Silvia Cartwright and a team of experts. The most illuminating document, however, is the publication which appeared in the *Journal of the American College of Obstetricians and Gynaecologists* dated October 1984., which tells of the 'Study reviews all of the 1028 women diagnosed histologically as having CIS (Carcinoma-in-situ.) of the cervix between January 1955 and December, 1976.'

The audacity of these people publishing a paper of a study which was clearly proved to have put the lives of 1028 women at risk. As we now know, several women actually died as a result of this 'witholding' of treatment. Where are the comparisons with the Liverpool incident apart from the obvious, the dates, and the fact that everyone 'sat back' and let it happen? Perhaps there are none, but surely it would seem reasonable, having looked at certain similarities, to ask whether or not something similar might not have been planned.

What if Dr. Lodge had been younger and might therefore have stayed on at the Women's Hospital for a number of years. Would the blunder have come to light when it did? I suggest it might not!

Dr. Lodge maintained throughout the inquiry that she had never seen the slides in question before. She speaks of her "wide experience in Cytopathology and Histopathology". She is indeed very experienced in her field. She actualy had a paper published some years ago, which is quite an achievement, as many papers are written each year for hopeful inclusion in the various medical journals, to actually get there is prestigous. She has enjoyed a most distinguished career beginning in 1945, and proceeding to gain further qualifications with commendations. She is certainly a well respected figure in the medical and scientific world and although some may describe her as 'formidable' there are six to one who would say otherwise, thinking most highly of her. I have met people who have worked with and trained under Dr. Lodge and they sing her praises. Bearing in mind that 'these people stick together' but even so, to this day they would not hestitate to ask her opinion and value it.

This doesn't sound like the same Dr. Lodge who was blamed for the Liverpool blunder. Who was found guilty of "a massive error of professional judgement", or was she guilty only because she was unable to offer the proof necessary to clear herself? What did she say to the review? I do not wish to make accusations. I can almost sympathise with her dilemma. She was of course, 'technically' guilty in that she was in charge of the laboratory, but I believe I have, in my effort to get to the truth, cast doubts on any real guilt. What a tragic end to a wonderful career, especially if doubt exists. My whole sympathy however, still remains with us, the women involved, because in casting doubt on the guilt of Dr. Lodge, we must now ask did she suspect something untoward was happening while she worked at the Women's? Was that why the allegation was raised? If so, did she also 'sit back' and let it happen? So many speculations! and so much room for more! That is what I dislike most about the entire affair.

Whatever the case may be I am not prepared to accept that she was guilty of a massive error of professional judgement'. With her experience, she would hardly have needed to give "more than a glance" to the very abnormal smears, some containing 'giant cells' although she may have had a conservative view of those containing 'minor' abnormalities. I have in my possession, a smear report, signed by Dr. Lodge during her term at the Women's, and correctly diagnosing a mild CIN.1 lesion. If she could assess this rather mild smear test correctly, then it would seem fairly impossible for her to misdiagnose several invasive cancer smears. I believe that she was a very convenient 'scapegoat'. We may never know what happened at the Women's Hospital during the period from March 1983 to December 1985, because the full report still remains hidden by the health authority. My latest efforts to gain access to that report following the death of another recall woman in December 1990, was met with point blank refusal

in a press statement issued by the authority spokesman to the effect that, "we will never allow Lily access to the full report and we will not meet with her to discuss any possibility of such. We will only meet with her to discuss women's health in general". Neither would there be a public inquiry. A strange statement from an authority who had earlier claimed that: "We have been very open with Lily, we have kept nothing back from her."
I had intended to take the matter further that time, but was impeded by the onset of the Gulf War.
You may wonder why it is so important to me that the truth be revealed, even after all this time. I can tell you in one word - *prevention!*
We must never allow this fiasco to happen again, because next time, there may be more deaths. We women complied with Government and Health Authority recommendations. We went along to have regular smears, and look what happened. We are sick to the teeth of hearing from those in power, "most of the women who die from cervical cancer have never had a smear". What we would most like to reply to that statement is this:
"911, (or was it 929?) Liverpool women did come in for a smear. We took responsibility for our health and well-being, and you let us down. And you further let us down by not allowing a public inquiry into a blunder which could have killed us all".

Afterword

As a result of Lily's speech at the Inaugural Meeting of the National Association of Cytologists in April 1990, she has been made the First Honorary Member of the Association.

Lily still runs her group, *CERCAN Women's Health Group* based in Liverpool.

If you have a problem with your smear test or cervical cancer, you can ring Lily on **051 525 2848** or write to her at:

CERCAN (Headquarters)
6, Landford Avenue
Liverpool L9 6BR

CERCAN (Group Meetings)
c/o Stockbridge Lane Community Centre
Stockbridge Lane,
Huyton,
Merseyside

CERCAN (Health Advice Shop)
c/o Sparrow Hall Community Council
38, Landford Avenue,
Liverpool L9 6BR

Authors Note

"I do not want any woman reading this to be put off from having a smear test. It is most important that we all have regular smears, because they can and do save lives. What you must beware of, is snags in the system. You should have a smear test every three years. You should make sure that you get your smear test results, and that you should be treated fairly quickly if you have an abnormal test. Don't forget, you cannot die from a CIN on your smear. This is an 'early morning alarm call' telling you that you may need treatment. The smear test can also find infections, so please don't worry if you have a positive result. Just ensure that you find out from your doctor exactly what is there.

"One other thing. If you are not satisfied with your smear test result, or you are worried about any aspect of smear testing, please do not suffer in silence. Seek help. There are many women's groups throughout the country who will be only too happy to give advice. Your local Community Health Council may have a list, or they may be able to help you."

Lily Hopkins

Lily and husband Chris when Lily was given the 'all-clear'

Lily and supporters campaigning for Legal Aid

Left to right: Donna Humphreys, James Fitzpatrick, Mr Criddall (Chief Administrator), Maria Partington and daughter, with Lily presenting her petition to Mr. Fitzpatrick

Left to right: Lily, Sylvia Sharpey-Schaffer (Liverpool Labour Councillor), Terry Fields MP accepting the letters addressed to all MPs